# MARK TWAIN

## A CHRISTIAN RESPONSE TO HIS BATTLE WITH GOD

First printing: September 2014

Master Books®, P.O. Box 726, Green Forest, AR 72638

Master Books® is a division of the New Leaf Publishing Group, Inc.

ISBN: 978-0-89051-845-8
Library of Congress Number: 2014949702

Cover by Diana Bogardus

Please consider requesting that a copy of this volume be purchased by your local library system.

**Printed in the United States of America**

Please visit our website for other great titles:
www.masterbooks.net

For information regarding author interviews,
please contact the publicity department at (870) 438-5288

Master
Books®
A Division of New Leaf Publishing Group
www.masterbooks.net

# CONTENTS

# INTRODUCTION

You are a famous writer and gifted speaker, living in the United States in the 19th century. You have written a book complaining that God has left the pleasures of sex out of His heaven, and that the deity in which you believe isn't the "malign thug" portrayed by the Bible.

But the society in which you live doesn't talk openly about sex, and such thoughts about God would be considered blasphemous. What are you to do? You have the book published one hundred years after your death, hoping that society would then be open-minded enough to listen.

Such was the foresight of inimitable and brilliant Mark Twain, whose philosophy about God and Christianity have sparked a revival of atheism and anti-Christian thinking across the world.

Mark Twain (1835–1910)
(Photo courtesy of Library of Congress)

# CHAPTER ONE

# THE NAKED COUPLE

It sounds surprising and almost heretical to say that the Bible opens its pages with a naked couple who were told by their Maker to have sex. But it's true. God made mankind naked as male and female, and He commanded them to be fruitful and multiply. And they happily complied. Ask a believer in evolution to explain the existence of male and female in elephants, horses, birds, fish, whales, giraffes, kangaroos, bears, fleas, flies, dogs, frogs, cats, bats, rats, and all 1.4 million different species of animals and they will be befuddled. As evidence of their befuddlement they will try to take you up a rabbit trail by pointing to a few snails and such that reproduce asexually. But the elephants are still in the room — both male and female.

If the entire universe is the result of nothing exploding into something, caused by nothing, why is it that almost every species has male and female, and they each reproduce after their own kind

. . . just as the Bible says? If you press skeptics, they will admit that they don't know. They will embrace intellectual insanity, hoping that someday someone will come up with a sane explanation — anything but that God created male and female and caused them to reproduce after their own kind. This is because every human being is born with a "carnal" mind that is in a state of "enmity" toward God.[1] That exists because shortly after Adam and Eve were created, sin entered the human race, and because we are human and are running the same race, we inherited a sinful, carnal, rebellious nature. The Bible says that we are "enemies of God" *in our minds* through wicked works (see Colossians 1:21).

This is never more evident than when blasphemy rolls off human lips. For millions, the prayer which says "hallowed be Thy name" has long been forgotten. Instead, "OMG" and "J---s Chr-st" are used to express disgust or said flippantly in a way that fails to give God's name due honor — from those in high public office, to celebrities in entertainment and music industries, to schoolchildren, to the man and woman on the street.

The enmity that finds expression through the mouth is deeply rooted in the human heart. The majority of Americans have some sort of belief in God, but until we find peace with Him we are offended by the God of the Bible — by His moral requirements and particularly by His judgments that are a consequence of those requirements. We don't want to be answerable to Him and will go to any lengths to shake off that uncomfortable yoke — like a wild steed that bucks in revolt when we are saddled with moral accountability. Anything that helps accomplish that is therefore highly prized by a sin-loving world.

**Dirt on God**

Mark Twain thought that he had found a lot of dirt on the God described in the Bible. If Mr. Twain could show that the God portrayed in Scripture was a morally bankrupt and merciless judge, then

---

1. "For to be carnally minded is death, but to be spiritually minded is life and peace. Because the carnal mind is enmity against God; for it is not subject to the law of God, nor indeed can be" (Romans 8:6–7).

the judgment spoken of so often in the Scriptures shouldn't take place. Humanity's case would be thrown out of court.

One example of his moral outrage was the pitiless judgments of God upon the Midianites. Although Twain doesn't give the source of the passage to which he refers (leaving no easy way for the thoughtful laymen to examine the legitimacy of his claims), he is clearly pointing to portions of the Book of Numbers:

> Then the LORD spoke to Moses, saying: "Harass the Midianites, and attack them; for they harassed you with their schemes by which they seduced you in the matter of Peor and in the matter of Cozbi, the daughter of a leader of Midian, their sister, who was killed in the day of the plague because of Peor" (Numbers 25:16–18).

God told Moses to declare war on the Midianites and to kill them. After the battle, Israel took the spoil:

> And the children of Israel took the women of Midian captive, with their little ones, and took as spoil all their cattle, all their flocks, and all their goods. They also burned with fire all the cities where they dwelt, and all their forts. And they took all the spoil and all the booty — of man and beast.
>
> Then they brought the captives, the booty, and the spoil to Moses, to Eleazar the priest, and to the congregation of the children of Israel, to the camp in the plains of Moab by the Jordan, across from Jericho. And Moses, Eleazar the priest, and all the leaders of the congregation, went to meet them outside the camp. But Moses was angry with the officers of the army, with the captains over thousands and captains over hundreds, who had come from the battle.
>
> And Moses said to them: "Have you kept all the women alive? Look, these women caused the children of Israel, through the counsel of Balaam, to trespass against the LORD in the incident of Peor, and there was a plague

among the congregation of the LORD. Now therefore, kill every male among the little ones, and kill every woman who has known a man intimately. But keep alive for yourselves all the young girls who have not known a man intimately (Numbers 31:9–18).

Here is Mark Twain's exposition of the above passage:

> Human history in all ages is red with blood, and bitter with hate, and stained with cruelties; but not since Biblical times have these features been without a limit of some kind. Even the Church, which is credited with having spilt more innocent blood, since the beginning of its supremacy, than all the political wars put together have spilt [this statement is no longer true, unless the First and Second World Wars could be considered religious and not political], has observed a limit. A sort of limit. But you notice that when the Lord God of Heaven and Earth, adored Father of Man, goes to war, there is no limit. He is totally without mercy — he, who is called the Fountain of Mercy. He slays, slays, slays! All the men, all the beasts, all the boys, all the babies; also all the women and all the girls, except those that have not been deflowered.
>
> He makes no distinction between innocent and guilty. The babies were innocent, the beasts were innocent, many of the men, many of the women, many of the boys, many of the girls were innocent, yet they had to suffer with the guilty. What the insane Father required was blood and misery; he was indifferent as to who furnished it.[2]

Then he explains what he believes happened with the virgins:

> The heaviest punishment of all was meted out to persons who could not by any possibility have deserved so horrible a fate — the 32,000 virgins. Their naked privacies

---

2. *Letters from the Earth*, "Letter XI," by Mark Twain, http://www.classicreader.com/book/1930/12/.

were probed, to make sure that they still possessed the hymen unruptured; after this humiliation they were sent away from the land that had been their home, to be sold into slavery; the worst of slaveries and the shamefulest, the slavery of prostitution; bed-slavery, to excite lust, and satisfy it with their bodies; slavery to any buyer, be he gentleman or be he a coarse and filthy ruffian.[3]

If what he is alleging actually took place, there would be no justification for such terrible humiliation. However, there is no validation for his belief that more than 32,000 woman were subjected to a medical examination to determine that they were virgins. Eastern cultures often indicated a woman's status. For example, Indian women wear a red "bindi" (a dot) to indicate that they are married. In biblical times, women wore a veil or jewelry, or they had certain hairstyles which indicated that they were married. This was because virginity was associated with legal proof for blood-inheritance issues in biblical times. Other women, such as prostitutes, also wore indicative clothing or jewelry (see Proverbs 7:10; Hosea 2:4–5). So it wasn't difficult to see those who still had their virginity, without this presumed medical examination.

**A Relevant Question**

Mark Twain clearly had a belief in God, despite claims to the contrary. He believed in a Creator. He said, "God puts something good and something lovable in every man His hands create."[4] But he qualified his belief in God. He said of the God of the Bible:

> I am plenty safe enough in his hands; I am not in any danger from that kind of a Diety. The one that I want to keep out of the reach of, is the caricature of him which one finds in the Bible. We (that one and I) could never respect each other, never get along together. I have met his superior

---

3. Ibid.
4. Albert Bigelow Paine, ed. *Mark Twain's Speeches*, "The American Vandal," 1868 (New York: Harper & Brothers, 1910), p. 29, http://twain.lib.virginia.edu/innocent/vandtext.html.

a hundred times — in fact I amount to that myself.[5] He also said, "Man proposes, but God blocks the game."[6]

So Mr. Twain was a theist. He believed in the existence of a Creator. Let me indulge time-travel for a moment and speak to him to make an important point:

> Mr. Twain, I know from your writings that you were not an atheist. You had a belief in God and this Deity is which you believe was different from the God of the Bible. That One is an offense to you. So here is my important question. Do you believe that the Bible is speaking the truth when it says, "The Lord said to Moses, treat the Midianites as enemies and kill them"? Did Almighty God actually *speak* to Moses? If you say you believe that He did, you have a problem. You are saying that the God — the Creator of the universe — your Creator and mine, supernaturally spoke from the heavens to Moses and told him to kill the Midianites. If that took place, you are admitting that the God revealed in the Old Testament is the one true God. He supernaturally spoke to Moses.
>
> On the other hand, if you are saying that the Old Testament is merely mythology, then why are you so indignant? Why are you irate about something that never happened? Again, either God spoke to Moses or He didn't. If He did, you have a problem, because He is therefore the true God and the Bible is the Word of God. If He didn't, you are outraged about something that never happened. That's like being angry at Cinderella's fairy godmother because she turned the carriage back into a pumpkin at midnight.
>
> Or do you think that the Bible is a myth and you are indignant because other people have a belief that's different from yours? Are you *that* intolerant of what others believe?

5. Caroline Thomas Harnesberger, ed. *Mark Twain at Your Fingertips*, Letter to Olivia Clemens, July 17, 1889 (New York: Beechurst Press, 1948), http://www.twainquotes.com/God.html.

6. Ibid.

Or perhaps you see yourself as the moral and intellectual savior of humanity and it's your job to tell them that their unthinking beliefs are inconsistent with good morals; morals such as yours. But who are you to say what is right and wrong? From where do you get your ethical standards? I would suggest that they trace themselves back to the Book you despise. The basis of your moral indignation is rooted in "Thou shalt not kill."

If you concede that God indeed spoke to Moses, then it's simply a matter of you standing in moral judgment over Almighty God. You think that God did something detestable, and you are pointing out the clear inconsistencies in His character. These are delusions of grandeur indeed for one sinful man, but they are not at all unusual thoughts for any human being, because our carnal minds are at enmity to God.

My questions to Mr. Twain are a little unfair because he cannot answer them. He went to meet his Maker way back in 1910. Nevertheless, before his demise he continued his tirade against the character of his Maker:

It was the Father that inflicted this ferocious and undeserved punishment upon those bereaved and friendless virgins, whose parents and kindred he had slaughtered before their eyes. And were they praying to him for pity and rescue, meantime? Without a doubt of it.

These virgins were "spoil" plunder, booty. He claimed his share and got it. What use had *he* for virgins? Examine his later history and you will know.

His priests got a share of the virgins, too. What use could priests make of virgins? The private history of the Roman Catholic confessional can answer that question for you. The confessional's chief amusement has been seduction — in all the ages of the Church. Père Hyacinth testifies that of a hundred priests confessed by him, ninety-nine had used the confessional effectively for the seduction of married women and young girls. One priest confessed that of nine hundred girls and women whom he had served as father and confessor in his time, none had escaped his lecherous embrace but the elderly and the homely. The official list of questions which the priest is required to ask will overmasteringly excite any woman who is not a paralytic.[7]

Mark Twain's contention for some reason moves away from God, and to the hypocrisy within the Roman Catholic Church, who he believed represented Him. Before I address this contention, I must say that the Protestant church also supposedly represents God, but that part of Christendom certainly isn't without sin either — with its many professed pastors who have been caught in sexual sin and the many slick preachers who have fleeced the flock through televangelism. But if Twain was offended by the Roman Catholic priests of his day, he would be horrified at what was uncovered in contemporary Catholicism. In recent years in the United States there have been more than 10,000 allegations of *pedophilia* among Catholic priests. Of these, 6,700 were investigated, and 1,872 priests were found guilty of molesting children.[8]

Thousands more cases were not investigated because those who were accused of pedophilia had died. Many other cases were reported in Ireland, Australia, New Zealand, Canada, Europe, Latin America, and Asia. These are commonly known and widely publicized facts.

Like Mark Twain, most people believe that Roman Catholicism is synonymous with biblical Christianity, and you can't blame them. Every Christmas and Easter the secular media parade the pope as being the leader of "the Christian Church." But ask most Catholics if they think that they are Christian, and they will answer, "No, I'm Roman Catholic." They know the difference between the two. For

---

7. *Letters from the Earth*, "Letter XI," by Mark Twain http://www.classicreader.com/book/1930/12/.

8. "Executive Summary of 'The Nature and Scope of Sexual Abuse of Minors by Catholic Priests and Deacons in the United States 1950–2002,' " *John Jay College of Criminal Justice* (Washington: United States Conference of Catholic Bishops, 2004).

example, Joseph Goebbels, Hitler's minister of propaganda, noted in his diary in 1939:

> The Fuehrer is deeply religious, but deeply anti-Christian. He regards Christianity as a symptom of decay. Rightly so. . . .[9]

Hitler told General Gerhart Engel:

> I am now as before a Catholic and will always remain so.[10]

Those who don't see the difference between Roman Catholic and Christian will often say that Adolf Hitler was a Christian, and those who don't know their Bibles (like Mark Twain) will often see hypocrisy in both Catholic and Protestant churches and blame God for the sins of man. They will blame the blood shed by the Roman Catholic Crusades and the Catholic Inquisitions upon the Christian Church.

Mark Twain then adds what he considers fuel to the fire in his case against God. He tells of an unsourced incident that is so horrific, so terribly cruel, it is hard contemplate:

> There is nothing in either savage or civilized history that is more utterly complete, more remorselessly sweeping than the Father of Mercy's campaign among the Midianites. The official report does not furnish the incidents, episodes, and minor details, it deals only in information in masses: *all* the virgins, *all* the men, *all* the babies, *all* "creatures *that breathe*," *all* houses, *all* cities; it gives you just one vast picture, spread abroad here and there and yonder, as far as eye can reach, of charred ruin and storm-swept desolation; your imagination adds a brooding stillness, an awful hush — the hush of death. But of course there were incidents. Where shall we get them?
>
> Out of history of yesterday's date. Out of history made by the Red Indian of America. He has duplicated God's

---

9. *Goebbels Diaries, 1939–1941,* 29 December 1939 (New York: Putnam, 1983).
10. John Toland, *Adolf Hitler* (New York: Anchor Publishing, 1992), p. 507.

work, and done it in the very spirit of God. In 1862 the Indians in Minnesota, having been deeply wronged and treacherously treated by the government of the United States, rose against the white settlers and massacred them; massacred all they could lay their hands upon, sparing neither age nor sex. Consider this incident:

> Twelve Indians broke into a farmhouse at daybreak and captured the family. It consisted of the farmer and his wife and four daughters, the youngest aged fourteen and the eldest eighteen. They crucified the parents; that is to say, they stood them stark naked against the wall of the living room and nailed their hands to the wall. Then they stripped the daughters bare, stretched them upon the floor in front of their parents, and repeatedly ravished them. Finally they crucified the girls against the wall opposite their parents, and cut off their noses and their breasts. They also — but I will not go into that. There is a limit. There are indignities so atrocious that the pen cannot write them. One member of that poor crucified family — the father — was still alive when help came two days later.

> Now you have one incident of the Minnesota massacre. I could give you fifty. They would cover all the different kinds of cruelty the brutal human talent has ever invented.[11]

This is why Twain said, "I have met his superior a hundred times — in fact I amount to that myself."[12] He considered himself to be morally superior to the cruel God portrayed in Scripture. His own image of the Creator (as opposed to the biblical portrayal) was more of a benevolent and lofty deity. This is what he said of this image in 1906:

11. *Letters from the Earth*, "Letter XI," by Mark Twain, http://www.classicreader.com/book/1930/12/.
12. Harnesberger, *Mark Twain at Your Fingertips*, Letter to Olivia Clemens, July 17, 1889, http://www.twainquotes.com/God.html.

Let us now consider the real God, the genuine God, the great God, the sublime and supreme God, the authentic Creator of the real universe, whose remotenesses are visited by comets only — comets unto which incredible distant Neptune is merely an outpost, a Sandy Hook to homeward-bound specters of the deeps of space that have not glimpsed it before for generations — a universe not made with hands and suited to an astronomical nursery, but spread abroad through illimitable reaches of space by the fiat of the real God just mentioned by comparison with whom the gods whose myriads infest the feeble imaginations of men are as a swarm of gnats scattered and lost in the infinitudes of the empty sky.[13]

His god was beyond human imagination, and was so remote that he didn't bother himself with the petty goings-on of humanity. Twain also said of his god:

I believe in God the Almighty.

I do not believe He has ever sent a message to man by anybody, or delivered one to him by word of mouth, or made Himself visible to mortal eyes at any time in any place.

I believe that the Old and New Testaments were imagined and written by man, and that no line in them was authorized by God, much less inspired by Him.

I think the goodness, the justice, and the mercy of God are manifested in His works: I perceive that they are manifested toward me in this life; the logical conclusion is that they will be manifested toward me in the life to come, if there should be one.

I do not believe in special providences. I believe that the universe is governed by strict and immutable laws. If one man's family is swept away by a pestilence and another

13. Albert Bigelow Paine, *Mark Twain, a Biography: The Personal and Literary Life of Samuel Langhorne Clemens*, Volume IV (New York: Harper & Brothers, 1912), p. 1582.

man's spared, it is only the law working: God is not inter-
fering in that small matter, either against the one man or in
favor of the other.[14]

Mark Twain believed in another god other than the One who
revealed Himself to Moses, and said, "I am the LORD your God. . . .
You shall have no other gods before Me" (Exodus 20:2–3).

Yet there is a serious inconsistency when it comes to his deity,
when it comes to the subject of human suffering. Twain was morally outraged that the God of the Bible was merciless, but his lofty
god also let that family suffer at the hands of those cruel Indians.
Why didn't his god show pity on them? He could have rescued
them, but he didn't bother. This is because he didn't interfere is
such small matters, "either against the one man or in favor of the
other." Besides being distant and heartless, his god created earthquakes that crush families. He also created killer tornados and terrifying hurricanes. He made poisonous spiders that bite, venomous vicious snakes, disease-carrying mosquitoes, man-eating lions
and sharks, fleas that bite dogs, dogs that bite cats, cats that bite
mice, and mice that spread plagues. Mark Twain's god created brain
cancer, lung cancer, throat cancer, cancer in kids, and the bacteria
that cause the horrific "flesh-eating" disease. He created heart disease, blindness, insanity, insomnia, depression, fear, thousands of
killer diseases, aging, and death. And then he coldly sits back on
some distant throne and has no interest in humanity.

Perhaps Mr. Twain should have thought a little deeper about
his own god's morality. On top of all the pain and suffering he created, he is so remote that he has no sense of truth or justice. He is
devoid of a sense of morality. This god sees all the evil in the world,
and like a corrupt judge, he turns a blind eye. Joseph Stalin was
responsible for the death of up to ten million people, and Twain's
god couldn't care less. Neither will Adolf Hitler be punished for
the genocide of six million Jews. The precious lives of all the Jewish
families mean nothing to him. When 49 headless bodies, including
6 women, were found on a highway in Mexico with their hands
and feet cut off, reportedly by the Mexican mafia, it was nothing

14. Ibid., p. 1583, http://twain.lib.virginia.edu/innocent/vandtext.html.

to the Twain-god. Women are raped, children are beaten and murdered, and it's no big deal because there is no Judgment Day nor heaven or hell.

The irony is that Twain once reiterated this oft-quoted phrase: "God created man in his own image and man, being a gentleman, returned the favor." Mark Twain's fertile imagination (his place of imagery) created his own immoral and heartless monster because the God of the Bible was offensive to him. And he did it for good reason.

# CHAPTER TWO

# MARK TWAIN AND SEX

Samuel Langhorne Clemens once wrote, "The human being, like the immortals, naturally places sexual intercourse far and away above all other joys — yet he has left it out of his heaven! The very thought of it excites him; opportunity sets him wild; in this state he will risk life, reputation, everything — even his queer heaven itself — to make good that opportunity and ride it to the overwhelming climax. From youth to middle age all men and all women prize copulation above all other pleasures combined, yet . . . it is not in their heaven; prayer takes its place."[1]

Few could deny the fact that presidents, politicians, priests, pastors, actors, and executives have forsaken fortunes, destroyed reputations, and revealed their true characters by diving and falling into

---

1. *Letters from the Earth*, "Letter II," by Mark Twain, http://www.classicreader.com/book/1930/3/.

sexual sin. King David fell off his lofty throne when he lusted after Bathsheba, and like a dumb sheep to the slaughter, lust led him by the nose to commit adultery and murder.

In August 2012, I was filming at a university when I saw two blind men standing on the sidewalk, so I asked if they would be willing to be interviewed on-camera. Both were in their mid-twenties and were totally blind. Juan was born without sight, and Feliciano lost his sight in a car accident. When I asked Juan to describe color for me, I thought he would be stumped. But he wasn't. He not only described what he perceived as "blue," he also described "green." As we discussed the Ten Commandments, he admitted to lying, stealing, and blasphemy. But when I began to say, "Jesus said, 'Whoever looks upon a woman to lust . . .'" suddenly, *I* was the one who was stumped. This man was born blind. *He had never even seen a woman!* I rephrased the question a little, and asked if he had had sexually impure thoughts about women, to which he enthusiastically replied that he had. The human heart doesn't need windows to let sin in. It's already there.

So there is no contention with the first part of Mark Twain's thoughts on man's insatiable lustful appetite. We all have it because of our sinful nature. However, his conclusions about the afterlife reveal a surprisingly shallow understanding about God and the Scriptures.

We need to continually remind ourselves that Mark Twain didn't believe the Bible. He didn't believe the Genesis account of man being made in God's image — that he was made with a sense of right and wrong. God created Adam in His likeness, and then He created a female. Again, He made them naked and left them in that state — along with the desire and the necessary paraphernalia to reproduce after their own kind. He no doubt made the woman attractive to Adam and He told them both to procreate. In other words, He commanded them to have sexual relations (to be fruitful and multiply), and in His great kindness He presumably made this a pleasurable experience. But Mr. Twain doesn't believe that account. He believed that the God revealed in Scripture was a thug.

## The Instruction Book for Sexual Relations

The Scriptures say of the woman:

> As a loving deer and a graceful doe, let her breasts satisfy
> you at all times; and always be enraptured with her love
> (Proverbs 5:19).

Why would the Bible *tell* a man to let his wife's breasts satisfy him
at all times? That's like telling a sport's fanatic to *let* his sport satisfy him at all times, when he already *loves* his sport. Perhaps it is
because God wants us to have a *guilt-free* sexual relationship. And
that's what we can have, if we are within the confines of the marital
bed . . . and according to the New Testament the marital bed is the
proposed place to have this intimate pleasure.[2]

American culture has a word to describe the feeling we get when
we have sexual desire (New Zealand, Australia, and England use a
different word that is a little less coarse-sounding). The Bible also
uses a word, and one that does seem more applicable than contemporary words. We say that dogs that are ready to mate are "in heat."
The Bible describes human beings in a similar way with the word
*burn*, saying, "It is better to marry than to burn" (1 Corinthians
7:9). The Amplified Bible puts it this way:

> But to the unmarried people and to the widows, I de-
> clare that it is well (good, advantageous, expedient, and
> wholesome) for them to remain single even as I do. But if
> they have not self-control (restraint of their passions), they
> should marry. For it is better to marry than to be aflame
> [with passion and tortured continually with ungratified de-
> sire] (1 Corinthians 7:8–9).

In other words, Christians should get married if they are in heat
— burning with sexual desire. Regular sexual relationships between
married couples keep the fire in control. So according to the Bible,
sex isn't something sinful, but rather a wonderful gift from God to
be thoroughly enjoyed within the boundaries of marriage. While a

---

2. See Hebrews 13:4.

blind world hasn't a clue why or how sex "evolved," we know that our Creator conceived the concept and His instruction Book tells us when and how to enjoy it:

> Let the husband render to his wife the affection due her, and likewise also the wife to her husband. The wife does not have authority over her own body, but the husband does. And likewise the husband does not have authority over his own body, but the wife does. Do not deprive one another except with consent for a time, that you may give yourselves to fasting and prayer; and come together again so that Satan does not tempt you because of your lack of self-control (1 Corinthians 7:3–5).

Scripture tells us that the only time a married couple should not have sex is when they are fasting, and that would seem to be for obvious reasons. So when Mark Twain railed on God for not having sex in heaven, we have to keep in mind that he didn't believe the Bible. He didn't believe that God created the paraphernalia for sex, that He made Adam and Eve naked and commanded them to have sex, that His Word tells us man is told to enjoy the breasts of his wife, that he should have sex with her in bed, and never let himself burn.

**Future Plans**

Put yourself in Adam's shoes (his bare feet) before sin entered the world. God has just created him from the dust of the earth. The newly formed man looks around at the amazing creatures in the Garden. His eyes take in the bright, colorful flowers, the mouth-watering fruit that hangs from beautiful trees, and plants that burst from the ground. Amazing birds, that make a peacock in full tail-spread look dull, walk around the garden. Birds, infinitely more fascinating than the most arrayed hummingbirds, fly between rich green plants and trees that have bright red and golden leaves.

This was before the Genesis Fall brought in the Curse. There were no dead leaves, weeds, thorns, rotting branches, or pest-eaten plants. There were no fleas, disease-carrying mosquitoes, scorpions, wasps, leeches, or filthy flies. There were no gophers digging holes in his Garden. Animals that were more majestic than lions, and others cuter than puppies, played together in the Garden. All food was pleasurable to the taste and turned into energy. Nothing turned into waste. Lions lay down with lambs. Lambs didn't become chops with gravy. The warm sun didn't burn Adam's tanned skin. The cool air was fresh without a drop of humidity, and no amount of expenditure caused Adam to sweat or become tired. He was incapable of experiencing depression, aging, sickness, or even pain. There was no such thing as sadness, boredom, or futility, and there was no death. He didn't get mauled by a bear, eaten by a tiger, bitten by a snake, struck by lightning, drowned by water, crushed by an earthquake, covered by an avalanche, or killed by a tornado. The Bible says that God saw it was "very good."[3] Those words were the understatement of eternity. Eden was perfection beyond words and even beyond human imagination.

God then tells Adam that He is going to create someone else who will be very similar to him, but with a few important modifications. This human being would be a different shape, slightly smaller, with a different facial design and a slightly different disposition. He would make Eve with the ability to reproduce Adam's children. She would be able to automatically create sons and daughters (the new model) for Adam, with a little of his help, which he wouldn't at all mind giving. Adam was going to like what God was about to create.

Although Adam could see what God had already done, do you think that he could have dreamed of what was on the assembly line? I don't think so. Think of the amazing animals that surround us — think of the patchwork-designed, super-long-necked giraffe, or the huge, bouncing Australian mouse with a front pocket, or the black and white stripped-down-sized horse, or the very slow mover that carries its home on its back. There are fish with wings, birds that fish, frogs that jump, and whales that send fountains of water into the heavens. Even in this fallen creation we see wonderful things and sights that no human mind could have begun to conceive, having never seen them before.

---

3. Genesis 1:31.

## Just Dust

Skeptics like to mock the thought that God made Adam from the dust of the earth. The next time someone mocks that thought, ask him how he thinks man was first made (don't complicate the issue by asking about the origin of women). Some think that perhaps there was a big bang and life came from non-life, which is a scientific impossibility. Most haven't a clue. It's a mystery, but that doesn't really worry them. They just know that God *didn't* make man from the dust of the earth. So the question to ask them is what is it that the body of a human being turns into after death. It decomposes and ends up as dust of the earth. God made man of the dust of the earth, breathed life into him, and when the life leaves, he goes back to dust. That's why preachers say from "dust to dust" at the funeral. Now there's a good clue for the clueless . . . if they want the mystery solved.

What is the alternative for those who prefer the evolutionary theory to Genesis? They either don't know, or they believe that there was nothing, and nothing created everything through a big bang. The heat from the bang sent massive rocks flying through space, and over time, non-life miraculously produced life, or the seeds of life were already on the rocks. Rocks produced human beings, animals, insects, and fish life — and all (as we have seen) produced male and female, each with the ability and specialized equipment to reproduce after their own kind.

A beautiful woman who outshined Hollywood's best could only have come from the infinitely creative mind of the wonderful Creator. Now hold these thoughts if you can! Not just the beautiful woman, but everything I have hopelessly tried to describe. Then couple those thoughts with the fact that the Scriptures tell us that our minds cannot *even begin* to imagine the wonderful, incredible, super-amazing, and everlasting pleasures that God has in store for those who love Him:

> But, on the contrary, as the Scripture says, What eye has not seen and ear has not heard and has not entered into the heart of man, [all that] God has prepared (made and

keeps ready) for those who love Him [who hold Him in affectionate reverence, promptly obeying Him and gratefully recognizing the benefits He has bestowed] (1 Corinthians 2:9; AMP).

If you think that the joys of this life are remarkable — snow-capped mountains, deep blue seas, beautiful flowers, amazing animals, delicious food, the marital bed (the pleasures of sex), color, love, and laughter — each one of them is less than nothing, compared to what God has waiting for those who love Him. But Mr. Twain didn't believe the Bible. He didn't believe that God created Adam or Eve. Consequentially, he looked at this fallen and cursed creation, with all its pain, suffering, and fleeting pleasures, and he thought that this is as things should be. He has no alternative, because the god he believed in was too lofty to give him any other explanation.

# CHAPTER THREE

# WHERE THERE'S SMOKE THERE'S NO FIRE

In *Letters from the Earth*, Twain bemoans human sexuality:

> The law of God, as quite plainly expressed in woman's construction is this: There shall be no limit put upon your intercourse with the other sex sexually, at any time of life. The law of God, as quite plainly expressed in man's construction is this: During your entire life you shall be under inflexible limits and restrictions, sexually. During twenty-three days in every month (in absence of pregnancy) from the time a woman is seven years old till she dies of old age, she is ready for action, and *competent*. . . . Competent every day, competent every night. Also, she . . . yearns for

it, longs for it, hankers after it, as commanded by the law of God in her heart (emphasis in original).[1]

"The law of God" is the decree that says that God made the woman this way (which those who believe Genesis know He didn't). The pains of menstruation and childbirth, aging, and death came as a result of the Genesis Curse. He then complains that men lose the ability to participate sexually after the age of 50. Most presume that this was his personal experience, because the society in which he lived didn't publicly speak of such things. Neither did Twain's generation know what we have now learned — that if a man takes carcinogens into his body they will in time take their toll in different ways.

## Mr. Dullbrain

Let me tell you about Mr. Dullbrain. He likes building smoke-billowing fires *inside* his house. He opens the windows every now and then to let in some fresh air when the smoke gets too thick. When asked why he keeps filling his house with poisonous smoke, he says that it makes him feel good. When concerned people tell him that if he keeps doing it, it will kill him, he says that he knows it will, but that he enjoys doing it so much he doesn't want to stop. Every time a fire goes out, he quickly lights another one to fill the house with thick toxic smoke.

Of course, it isn't long until he becomes deathly sick as a result of the carcinogens in the smoke he so loves. As he lay on his deathbed with a look of horror in his eyes, gasping for every breath, he begins to realize what a fool he has been. Mr. Dullbrain was aptly named.

Mark Twain loved to fill his house with smoke. He smoked like an over-stoked train. He said,

> I began to smoke immoderately when I was eight years old; that is, I began with one hundred cigars a month, and by the time I was twenty I had increased my allowance to two

---

1. *Letters from the Earth*, "Letter VIII," by Mark Twain, http://www.classicreader.com/book/1930/9/.

Mark Twain
(Photo courtesy of Library of Congress)

hundred a month. Before I was thirty, I had increased it to three hundred a month. I think I do not smoke more than that now; I am quite sure I never smoke less.[2]

He experimented with a time of not smoking, but lit the fires again because he found that the smoke helped him write:

I was three weeks writing six chapters. Then I gave up the fight, resumed my three hundred cigars, burned the six

---

2. A. Arthur Reade, ed. *Study and Stimulants; or, The Use of Intoxicants and Narcotics in Relation to Intellectual Life, As Illustrated by Personal Communications on the Subject, From Men of Letters and of Science* (Manchester: Abel Heywood and Son, 1883), p. 121.

chapters, and wrote the book in three months, without any bother or difficulty . . . consequently, I ordinarily smoke fifteen cigars during my five hours' labors, and if my interest reaches the enthusiastic point, I smoke more. I smoke with all my might, and allow no intervals.[3]

He probably did get some sort of mental high through his smoking, which would explain why his thoughts about God and the Bible were so clouded. The brain is connected directly to the heart and the lungs through arteries. These arteries carry oxygen and other chemicals to the brain. So, when a person inhales smoke, the chemicals are sent directly to the brain within ten seconds and can remain active for up to 40 minutes.

Studies on smoking have found that men who smoke are more prone to impotence:

If heart disease, stroke and certain cancers haven't been reason enough for men to quit smoking, consider this: The habit also increases the risk of erectile dysfunction. In fact, emerging research shows that men with a pack-a-day habit are almost 40 percent more likely to struggle with erectile dysfunction than men who don't smoke.[4]

As he sucked in the carcinogens, Twain bragged of his continued health. He didn't think of the consequences of consuming huge amounts of poisonous chemicals. He boasted,

I am forty-six years old, and I have smoked immoderately during thirty-eight years, with the exception of a few intervals, which I will speak of presently. During the first seven years of my life I had no health — I may almost say that I lived on allopathic medicine, but since that period I have hardly known what sickness is. My health has been excellent, and remains so.[5]

3. Ibid, p. 122.
4. Serena Gordon, "Men Who Smoke Prone to Impotence," *HealthDay News*, December 2012, http://abcnews.go.com/Health/Healthday/story?id=4509892&page=1.
5. Reade, *Study and Stimulants*, p. 120–121.

## The Christian's House

Common sense tells us that a low-grade fuel will not yield a high performance in any vehicle. However, those who believe and obey the Bible find instructions on how to get the best performance:

> For bodily exercise profits a little, but godliness is profitable for all things, having promise of the life that now is and of that which is to come. This is a faithful saying and worthy of all acceptance (1 Timothy 4:8–9).

It is because the Christians belong to God that they honor Him in all they do. We take care of the "house" through regular exercise and healthy eating, and that means, among other things, not filling it with smoke. Sensible living has a *natural* benefit in this life, and godliness has a *supernatural* benefit in the life to come. This can be seen in the life of Abraham, who had the ability and benefit of enjoying sexual pleasure into his late nineties:

> [For Abraham, human reason for] hope being gone, hoped in faith that he should become the father of many nations, as he had been promised, So [numberless] shall your descendants be.
>
> He did not weaken in faith when he considered the [utter] impotence of his own body, which was as good as dead because he was about a hundred years old, or [when he considered] the barrenness of Sarah's [deadened] womb (Romans 4:18–19; AMP).

But we know that Mr. Twain didn't believe Abraham way outlasted him, because he didn't believe the Bible. He preferred to believe that instead of enjoying pleasure forevermore, we will be kneeling in prayer for eternity. What do you believe? Do you believe the promises of the Scriptures? Look at what they say:

> You will show me the path of life; in Your presence is fullness of joy; at Your right hand are pleasures forevermore (Psalm 16:11).

Notice the word "forevermore." The pleasure the godly are promised is *everlasting*. We will live in a world without end. Here's another promise from the Word of God:

> So the ransomed of the LORD shall return,
> And come to Zion with singing,
> With everlasting joy on their heads.
> They shall obtain joy and gladness;
> Sorrow and sighing shall flee away (Isaiah 51:11).

The word "joy" sounds a little trite to the worldly man. However, it is joy that he is seeking every time he attempts to en-joy (put joy in) himself. Those who trust in Jesus are promised *everlasting* joy. There's a reason the Scriptures so often mention the eternality of pleasure. This is because every pleasure we experience on this earth is transient. It doesn't last, and afterward we are left looking for more. Whether it's the pleasures of sex, laughter with friends or family, the enjoyment of good food, the excitement of some sport — all of it is like water in our hands. It falls through our fingers no matter how much we try to hold onto it. It is gone in a moment of time and becomes like a faded photo in the memory that senility eventually rips in two.

King Solomon concluded that the pleasures we chase in this life are like the futility of chasing the wind, and he certainly chased pleasures. Speaking of the king's sexual exploits, Mr. Clemens said,

> Solomon, who was one of the Deity's favorites, had . . . seven hundred wives and three hundred concubines. To save his life he could not have kept two of these young creatures satisfactorily refreshed, even if he had fifteen experts to help him. Necessarily almost the entire thousand had to go hungry for years and years on a stretch. Conceive of a man hardhearted enough to look daily upon all that suffering and not be moved to mitigate it.[6]

---

6. *Letters from the Earth*, "Letter VIII," by Mark Twain, http://www.classicreader.com/book/1930/9/

Solomon, with all that pleasure, realized life's dilemma. It is futile. The consolation we have is the knowledge that this futile existence isn't the way things should be. Again, when Adam sinned, he brought about the Genesis Curse, which ushered in futility, disease, pain, suffering, and death. God subjected the entire creation to futility because of that one sinful act of rebellion:

> For the creation was subjected to futility, not willingly, but because of Him who subjected it in hope; because the creation itself also will be delivered from the bondage of corruption into the glorious liberty of the children of God. For we know that the whole creation groans and labors with birth pangs together until now. Not only that, but we also who have the firstfruits of the Spirit, even we ourselves groan within ourselves, eagerly waiting for the adoption, the redemption of our body (Romans 8:20–23).

The whole of creation groans because of the Curse. Earthquakes, floods, hurricanes, tornadoes, etc., continually rock this earth. Animals, fish, birds, and insects devour each other. In time, the most beautiful of women fade like a withered leaf, become old and die. So do handsome (and not-so-handsome) men. So do birds, fish, dogs, cats, elephants, fleas, and trees. We all whither and decline because of the Genesis Curse, and as Christians, we groan as we wait for the promised new immortal body that God can now legally give us because Jesus reversed the Curse. He satisfied the anger of God against wicked humanity. He took our punishment upon Himself, and that meant that God could lawfully commute our death sentence and let us live. He could freely give us pleasure that never ends.

We have the promise of eternal life from the One who made all the wonderful things we see in creation. All we need do is repent and trust in Jesus to experience the reality of that promise. What incredible love God has for sinful humanity. How unspeakably kind and merciful He is. But Mr. Twain didn't believe that the God revealed in Scripture is kind. He called Him a "thug."

## The Skeleton in the Closet

As we read the New Testament, we see that the religious leaders at the time of Christ were like whitewashed tombs. They were pure on the outside but inside there was a pile of skeletons. Like an indignant self-righteous Pharisee robed in pure white, Mark Twain continually denounced the immorality of God, but did so privately.

> Mark Twain was obsessed with his legacy, and he was determined to create an edifice that would withstand fickle readers and prying critics and forever establish him as America's greatest writer. . . . He was aided in his task by his hand-picked biographer, Albert Bigelow Paine, who opined that no one should ever be allowed to write about Twain: "As soon as this is begun (writing about him at all, I mean) the Mark Twain that we have 'preserved' . . . the traditional Mark Twain — will begin to fade and change, and with that process the Harper Mark Twain property will depreciate." Paine need not have worried. The "property" has maintained its popularity. A century later, the white-suited, genteel figure of the elderly Twain remains one of the most recognizable figures in American culture.[7]

That's what Mark Twain came to be revered as — an honest, moral, straight shooter. However, his robe may not be as clean as it seems. Laura Skandera Trombley, author of *Mark Twain's Other Woman: The Hidden Story of His Final Years*, says of his three-volume autobiography published in 2010:

> The third volume will reportedly include a 429-page blackmail manuscript that Twain spent five of the last 12 months of his life writing, a manuscript that he never intended for publication. Twain's hoots of delight would instantly cease if he knew readers would soon be exposed

---

7. Laura Skandera Trombley, "Mark Twain's Sex Toys," June 9, 2010, www.thedailybeast.com/articles/2010/06/09/mark-twains-sex-toys-and-legacy.html.

to the "Ashcroft-Lyon Manuscript." The object of Twain's wrath was Isabel Van Kleek Lyon, his social secretary and companion for six and a half years.[8]

The "Ashcroft-Lyon Manuscript" reveals another side of the pure and eloquent moralist.[9]

He accused Isabel of repeatedly trying to seduce him, although he maintained that he refused to give in to her advances. Twain eventually fired his mistress. He then called her "a drunkard, a sneak, a humbug, a traitor, a conspirator, a filthy-minded and salacious slut pining for seduction and always getting disappointed, poor child."[10] He threatened to publish the manuscript, destroying her reputation, if she told anyone.

His autobiography reveals proof of Mark Twain's lifelong animosities and his predilection toward protecting his public persona:

> This means that the general public and Twain scholars will need to reassess someone they thought they knew (and defended) so well. The whitewashed version of an asexual old man that has been in place for a century is passé. The time has come to rethink Mark Twain. . . .[11]

One book reviewer speaks further of Twain's image of supposed high morals, and of his iconic status coming unglued by the truth:

> I'll admit that I read *Mark Twain's Other Woman* because of its hint at a dark side to Mark Twain's sexuality. Here is a man we have come to consider the ultimate American, a hero with the high morals of another era. And of course we would: Twain was careful to construct his own life history before his death in 1910. In fact, he dictated his biography himself. *Mark Twain's Other Woman* tells a different tale than the authorized biography — one presented through

---

8. Ibid.
9. Ibid.
10. Ibid.
11. Ibid.

the eyes of his second-to-last personal secretary, Isabel Van Kleek Lyon.[12]

Reviewer Tom Mackin noted that the "tale of Twain's social secretary unearths author's ugly side":

> Lost in this melancholy story of greed, adultery and blackmail are Huckleberry Finn, Tom Sawyer, Pudd'nhead Wilson and the other beloved characters from the late 19th century who made Samuel Langhorne Clemens (Mark Twain) one of the most important American writers. Yet one can no more stop reading this tragic book than one can stop watching a train wreck.
>
> Unfortunately, when the wreckage is cleared, Twain is revealed to be a man obsessed with self-promotion, wealth and protecting the reputation of his daughters. . . .[13]

It seems that Mr. Twain was revealing something about *himself* when he said,

> Everybody lies — every day; every hour; awake; asleep; in his dreams; in his joy; in his mourning; if he keeps his tongue still, his hands, his foes, his eyes, his attitude, will convey deception — and purposely.[14]

Samuel Clemens lived a lie. He wasn't the man he wanted us to think he was. He was like the rest of us, except for the fact that he thought himself to be more moral than Almighty God. He was obsessed with his legacy. His attitude was similar to his smoking. He continually sucked in masses not thinking of the eventual

---

12. Jeanine Birong, "'Mark Twain's Other Woman': A Creepy Two-Timer, But Still a Great Read," Greater Long Beach, August 12, 2010. www.greaterlongbeach.com/12/08/2010/mark-twains-other-woman-a-creepy-two-timer-maybe-but-still-a-great-read.

13. Star-Ledger Staff, "'Mark Twain's Other Woman' book review: Tale of Twain social secretary unearths author's ugly side," March 21, 2010; NJ.com, www.nj.com/entertainment/arts/index.ssf/2010/03/mark_twains_other_woman_book_r.html.

14. Mark Twain, "On the Decay of the Art of Lying," 1882, The Literature Network. www.online-literature.com/twain/1320.

consequences. He should have been more concerned about his eternity, rather than his legacy:

> Therefore you are inexcusable, O man, whoever you are who judge, for in whatever you judge another you condemn yourself; for you who judge practice the same things. But we know that the judgment of God is according to truth against those who practice such things. And do you think this, O man, you who judge those practicing such things, and doing the same, that you will escape the judgment of God? (Romans 2:1–3).

But there is a double tragedy when a man is blinded by godless thoughts. The Psalmist said, "Your Word is a lamp to my feet and a light to my path" (Psalm 119:105). Mark Twain snuffed out this God-given light, leaving him in darkness as to life's purpose, instructions on how to live, how to find everlasting life, and what is to come.

## The Defense

When well-known atheist Christopher Hitchens was asked, "If God does not exist, what then is the purpose of life?" he responded:

> Well, I can only answer for myself. What cheers me up? I suppose mainly gloating over the misfortunes of other people. Mainly crowing over the miseries of others. It doesn't always work but it never completely fails. And then there's irony, which is the gin in the Campari, the cream in the coffee. Sex can have diminishing returns but it's amazing . . . that's pretty much it; then it's a clear run to the grave.[15]

Hitchens was sometimes blatantly honest. Like most unregenerate men, he lived for pleasure and he dealt with guilt by the foolishness of atheism. He also smoked like a train and died of throat cancer. He lived without concern for consequences.

---

15. "Wishing Tony Judt Well," January 10, 2010; www.christopherhitchenswatch. blogspot.com/2010/01/wishing-tony-judt-well.html.

Mark Twain dealt with his guilt through idolatry rather than the impossibility of atheism. When he thought about the God of the Bible, like Adam when caught in his transgression, Twain shifted the blame from himself to God:

> I wish I could learn to remember that it is unjust and dishonorable to put blame upon the human race for any of its acts. For it did not make itself, it did not make its nature, it is merely a machine, it is moved wholly by outside influences, it has no hand in creating the outside influences nor in choosing which of them it will welcome or reject, its performance is wholly automatic, it has no more mastership nor authority over its mind than it has over its stomach, which receives material from the outside and does as it pleases with it, indifferent to its proprietor's suggestions, even, let alone his commands; wherefore, whatever the machine does — so called crimes and infamies included — is the personal act of its Maker, and He, solely, is responsible.[16]

Again, he wasn't foolish enough to think that the human race made itself. He knew that we had "no hand in creating." He also believed that we have no more control over our mind than we have over the stomach. While it's true that the stomach works independently of the will, we are the ones who choose the food that goes into the mouth and into it.

We feed the mind. We choose thoughts that we enjoy chewing over, and if those thoughts transgress God's Law, then we are morally accountable to the God who considers lust to be adultery (see Matthew 5:27–28). While some may swallow Twain's foolish attempts to blame God for all human "acts," it makes no sense when we think a little. Many a rapist or murderer has tried the "God made me do it" defense, and if it doesn't work in a court of law, it's not going to work on Judgment Day.

---

16. Albert Bigelow Paine, ed., *Mark Twain's Letters* (New York: Harper & Brothers, 1917), p. 763–764.

# CHAPTER FOUR

# TWAIN, FLIES, AND EVOLUTION

Mark Twain was like a man on a sinking ship. The captain has instructed the passengers to stay calm and get into the lifeboats, but instead of doing as he's been told, he stands on a soapbox between the lifeboats and the passengers, and maligns the character of the captain. He blames the captain for the predicament, despite his evident compassion in telling the passengers how they can be saved.

To bolster his case against the captain, he points to the hole in the ship's side and the water pouring in. He points to the injuries of the passengers who fell because of the initial impact that caused the ship to begin to sink. It's as though he so hates the captain he refuses to believe the ship is even sinking, and yet at the same time he points to all the signs that it's sinking. He prefers to perish by drowning, and he wants to take as many people down with him as he can.

Every human being is going to die. The ship is sinking and taking all of us down with it. We know that God has graciously given us His Word and it tells us that to be saved we must trust the Savior — the one called "The Captain of our Salvation." The Bible tells us that we will die because we live in a fallen creation — filled with disease, suffering, and death. All around us we see the truth of this statement — thousands of terrible diseases, earthquakes, draughts, hurricanes, tornadoes, snakes and spiders that have a deadly bite, disease-ridden, biting mosquitoes, filthy cockroaches, etc. When God cursed the earth, it was exceptionally exhaustive. Murphy's Law is a reality. What can go wrong, does go wrong. And it's been wrong since the Fall. The *whole* of creation is diseased and is devouring itself as the Scriptures say. Every part of it is "groaning."

All of our terrible suffering — from hemorrhoids to migraines, mouth ulcers, stomach ulcers, epileptic fits, birth pains, brain cancer, thousands of horrific and debilitating diseases, and death — is overwhelming evidence that the Bible is correct when it informs us that we are in a fallen state and that we are in rebellion to our Creator.

But instead of believing the Scriptures, Twain uses all the signs of a fallen creation to mock and accuse God and the Bible. With a burning evangelistic zeal, he uses his soapbox to try to turn as many people as he can from coming to the only One who can give them everlasting life.

Take, for example, Twain's diatribe on God, as he wrongly concludes that God made the fly in its present filthy state:

> There is much inconsistency concerning the fly. In all the ages he has not had a friend, there has never been a person in the earth who could have been persuaded to intervene between him and extermination; yet billions of persons have excused the Hand that made him — and this without a blush.[1]

---

1. John S. Tuckey, ed., *The Devil's Race-track: Mark Twain's Great Dark Writings* (Berkeley and Los Angeles, CA: University of California Press, 1966), p. 19.

Again, those who believe the Scriptures do not "excuse" God for creating the filthy fly, or the filthy mosquito, or the filthy cockroach. The state of these insects and all the biting, devouring, diseased vicious animals are because of the Fall. But Mr. Clemens doesn't believe that, and so he flies off the handle about the fly, when what he says flies in the face of reason, in the light of Holy Scripture:

> Would they have excused a Man in the same circumstances, a man positively known to have invented the fly? . . . Let us try to think the unthinkable: let us try to imagine a Man of a sort willing to invent the fly; that is to say, a man destitute of feeling; a man willing to wantonly torture and harass and persecute myriads of creatures who had never done him any harm and could not if they wanted to, and — the majority of them — poor dumb things not even aware of his existence. In a word, let us try to imagine a man with so singular and so lumbering a code of morals as this: that it is fair and right to send afflictions upon the just — upon the unoffending as well as upon the offending, without discrimination. If we can imagine such a man, that is the man that could invent the fly, and send him out on his mission and furnish him his orders: "Depart into the uttermost corners of the earth, and diligently do your appointed work. Persecute the sick child; settle upon its eyes, its face, its hands, and gnaw and pester and sting; worry and fret and madden the worn and tired mother who watches by the child, and who humbly prays for mercy and relief with the pathetic faith of the deceived and the unteachable."[2]

The fly is an annoying, horrible, diseased pest. It is a curse, and he is mad at the God of the Bible for making it, even though he doesn't believe that the God of the Bible made it. Why doesn't he blame his god — the one we have seen in which Mark Twain believes? Yet he

---

2. Ibid., p. 19–20.

insists on blaming the God of the Scriptures for the fly (and everything he considers to be evil) and refuses to give Him thanks for everything that is good. He should give God thanks for his beloved wife and children, for his daily food, his health, his freedom, for his sharp and witty mind. Instead, he used his wit to vilify the One who gave Him every blessing of life. He insisted on biting the Hand that fed him. He even mocks God's incredible patience, love, and kindness:

> We hear much about His patience and forbearance and long-suffering; we hear nothing about our own, which much exceeds it. We hear much about His mercy and kindness and goodness — in words — the words of His Book and of His pulpit — and the meek multitude is content with this evidence, such as it is, seeking no further; but whoso searcheth after a concreted sample of it will in time acquire fatigue. There being no instances of it.[3]

Then he once again accuses Almighty God of immorality. He accuses Him of inaction when it comes to helping humanity, calling the preacher a trained "parrot in the pulpit" and those that listen to him "a trained congregation." Mark Twain steps in as the intellectual savior for these poor fools who haven't the ability (as he has) to think, and therefore see through the fraud of Christianity. Again, pulpit parrots and their listeners simply believe Genesis and understand why suffering exists, and because they know the Scriptures, they trust God's integrity, faithfulness, and His ability to deliver them from the sinking ship. Yet Samuel Clemens sees their thoughts and motives and judges them fools:

> It is plain that there is one moral law for heaven and another for the earth. The pulpit assures us that wherever we see suffering and sorrow which we can relieve and do not do it, we sin, heavily. . . . Nevertheless we have this curious spectacle: daily the trained parrot in the pulpit gravely delivers himself of these ironies, which

3. Ibid., p. 21.

he has acquired at second-hand and adopted without examination, to a trained congregation which accepts them without examination, and neither the speaker nor the hearer laughs at himself.[4]

After dismissing Christians as unthinking fools, he turns his thoughts to the subject of evolution:

> Adam is fading out. It is on account of Darwin and that crowd. I can see that he is not going to last much longer. There's a plenty of signs. He is getting belittled to a germ — a little bit of a speck that you can't see without a microscope powerful enough to raise a gnat to the size of a church. They take that speck and breed from it: first a flea; then a fly, then a bug, then cross these and get a fish, then a raft of fishes, all kinds, then cross the whole lot and get a reptile, then work up the reptiles till you've got a supply of lizards and spiders and toads and alligators and Congressmen and so on, then cross the entire lot again and get a plant of amphibiums, which are half-breeds and do business both wet and dry, such as turtles and frogs and ornithorhyncuses and so on, and cross-up again and get a mongrel bird, sired by a snake and dam'd by a bat, resulting in a pterodactyl, then they develop *him*, and water his stock till they've got the air filled with a million things that wear feathers, then they cross-up all the accumulated animal life to date and fetch out a mammal, and start-in diluting again till there's cows and tigers and rats and elephants and monkeys and everything you want down to the Missing Link, and out of him and a mermaid they propagate Man, and there you are![5]

So does he believe Darwin's theory or doesn't he? He makes evolution sound like the joke that it is by describing it in one breathtaking 190-word sentence. He maintains it makes no sense, saying he's thought it over, and he sided with Adam:

---

4. Ibid., p. 21–22.
5. Tuckey, *The Devil's Race-track*, p. 340–341.

Well, then, was it? To my mind, it don't stand to reason. They say it took a hundred million years. Suppose you ordered a Man at the start, and had a chance to look over the plans and specifications — which would you take, Adam or the germ? Naturally you would say Adam is business, the germ ain't; one is immediate and sure, the other is speculative and uncertain. Well, I have thought these things all over, and my sympathies are with Adam. Adam was like *us*, and so he seems near to us, and dear. He is kin, blood kin, and my heart goes out to him in affection. But I don't feel that way about that germ. The germ is too far away — and not only that, but such a wilderness of reptiles between. . . . Very well, then, where do we arrive? Where do we arrive with our respect, our homage, our filial affection? At Adam! At Adam, every time.[6]

He then seems confused about the time it took for man to evolve, and about the age of the earth:

Man has been here 32,000 years. That it took a hundred million years to prepare the world for him is proof that that is what it was done for. I suppose it is. I dunno. If the Eiffel Tower were now representing the world's age, the skin of paint on the pinnacle-knob at its summit would represent man's share of that age; and anybody would perceive that that skin was what the tower was built for. I reckon they would, I dunno.[7]

He then describes evolution as an unplanned, self-creating, self-perpetuating snowball that ends up looking as though it was planned:

Evolution is a blind giant who rolls a snowball down a hill. The ball is made of flakes — circumstances. They contribute to the mass without knowing it. They adhere

---

6. Ibid., p. 341.
7. Mark Twain, *Letters from the Earth*, "The Damned Human Race" (New York: Fawcett World Library, 1966), p. 170.

without intention, and without foreseeing what is to result. When they see the result they marvel at the monster ball and wonder how the contriving of it came to be originally thought out and planned. Whereas there was no such planning, there was only a law: the ball once started, all the circumstances that happened to lie in its path would help to build it, in spite of themselves.[8]

Evolution is senseless, and ridiculous. It should be ridiculed because it makes no sense. I penned this poem in honor of Charles Darwin:

> *Darwin's Gift to Humanity*
> My name is insomnia, I keep you from sleep
> I want to make you miserable; I want to make you weep
> If you get away from me, I have a good friend
> His name is Night-terrors and he will get you in the end
>
> To wake up with the sweats with darting wide eyes
> Panting and shaking with deep painful sighs
> I also have friends called Sickness and Pain
> Whose job is to kill you or injure or maim
>
> They have small annoyances, like itches and aches
> They want you to suffer and will do what it takes
> There's deafness and blindness and fears from within
> That drive to the false refuge of whiskey and gin
>
> There are pains in the neck and pains in the back
> There are pains in head and pains that attack
> The liver, the kidneys, the lungs and the heart
> There are pains in the bladder that strike like a dart
>
> There's heartburn and acid that comes from the gut
> And earache and toothache and pains from a cut
> There's asthma, arthritis and a whole lot more
> Terrifying diseases to put you at death's dark door

---

8. David Ketterer, ed., *Mark Twain: Tales of Wonder*, "The Secret History of Eddypus," (Lincoln, NE: University of Nebraska Press, 1984), p. 222–223.

There are ailments with names that are real hard to say
That are attacking and maiming thousands each day
There's frightening cancers that eat at the brain
And others so painful they will drive you insane

So what hope can you give me if the fittest survive?
The hopelessness of evolution can't keep me alive
It's unscientific, and was dreamed up by man
Who runs from his Creator whenever he can

We live in a world that has fallen from God
And when we feel these pains we should give a wise nod
And believe the Scriptures despite what men say
Who will stand before God and believe on that Day

They will get what they deserve, they loved lying and lust
And despised the cross and repentance and trust
They will wish that we warned them that God meant
       what He said
But swallowed the lie, when men are dead, they're dead

If you're not born again, please listen to me
God offers eternal life, and it's completely free
Don't ignore the warnings of life's pains anymore
Because this place is Heaven compared to what's in store

I'm speaking the truth and deep down you know it
Life is most precious; make sure you don't blow it
God so loved the world, He gave Jesus His Son
You don't need religion because the sufferings been done

So go save the whales and look after the trees
Lay off the salt and don't eat too much cheese
Eat plenty of fiber and die healthy and well
But die in your sins, and you will end up in hell.

# CHAPTER FIVE

# LITTLE BESSIE'S BIG LIES

In 1908, Samuel Clemens wrote "Little Bessie,"[1] a discourse between a three-year-old child and her "Christian" mother. Little Bessie is a puppet through which Mr. Clemens once again airs his anger against the God of the Bible, in whom he doesn't believe. He seemed to think that his arguments would be more readily believed if they were presented through the wide eyes of an innocent child. However, there is a serious disconnect between Twain and reality. Bessie is barely three years old! The theological dialogue would have perhaps been credible if she had been seven or eight years of age. This out of touch with real life is also seen by his conviction that a female child was ready for sex at seven years old, as mentioned earlier. While

---

1. "Little Bessie," by Mark Twain, from *Fables of Man,* John S. Tuckey, editor, University of California Press, 1972; http://www.positiveatheism.org/hist/ twainbes.htm.

other three-year-olds were playing with dolls and learning to hold a spoon, Bessie was "meditative" and "thoughtful" in her philosophy of life's enigmas.

I will quote the entirety of its six short chapters (for contextual integrity) and look closely at Twain's twisting of truth through little Bessie:

Chapter 1
*Little Bessie Would Assist Providence*

Little Bessie was nearly three years old. She was a good child, and not shallow, not frivolous, but meditative and thoughtful, and much given to thinking out the reasons of things and trying to make them harmonize with results. One day she said —

"Mamma, why is there so much pain and sorrow and suffering? What is it all for?"

It was an easy question, and mamma had no difficulty in answering it:

"It is for our good, my child. In His wisdom and mercy the Lord sends us these afflictions to discipline us and make us better."

"Is it *He* that sends them?"

"Yes."

"Does He send *all* of them, mamma?"

"Yes, dear, all of them. None of them comes by accident; He alone sends them, and always out of love for us, and to make us better."

"Isn't it strange!"

"Strange? Why, no, I have never thought of it in that way. I have not heard any one call it strange before. It has always seemed natural and right to me, and wise and most kindly and merciful."

"Who first thought of it like that, mamma? Was it you?"

"Oh, no, child, I was taught it."

"Who taught you so, mamma?"

"Why, really, I don't know — I can't remember. My mother, I suppose; or the preacher. But it's a thing that everybody knows."

"Well, anyway, it does seem strange. Did He give Billy Norris the typhus?"

"Yes."

"What for?"

"Why, to discipline him and make him good."

"But he died, mamma, and so it *couldn't* make him good."

## Lie One: God disciplines us to make us good

This is not true. God doesn't discipline anyone to make him or her good. Twain may have believed that it was so, but he was wrong. Had he taken the time to study the Bible he wouldn't have misrepresented one of its most basic truths — justification.

The moment a sinner repents and trusts in the Savior, he is justified in the sight of God. He is made righteous through His amazing grace (see Ephesians 2:8–9). This happens in an instant of time. The righteousness of Christ is credited to his bankrupt account. He was morally in debt to the Law, under its fierce wrath, but Jesus paid the fine in full. But the guilty criminal's case was dismissed because of more than a lack of evidence. It was terminated because of no evidence at all. Guilty though the sinner is because of a multitude of sins, they were all washed away the second he or she repented and trusted alone in Jesus.

So a Christian is morally perfect in the eyes of God. He doesn't see a sinner. Instead, He looks upon the imputed righteousness of Christ, and any of life's trials that then come a Christian's way happen for his good (see Romans 8:28). They don't happen to *make* him good, because he is already "good" in the biblical sense (morally perfect). For Mr. Twain to say such a thing is to seriously misrepresent the Christian faith, slur the character of God, and to perpetuate a lie.

"Well, then, I suppose it was for some other reason. We know it was a *good* reason, whatever it was."

"What do you think it was, mamma?"

"Oh, you ask so many questions! I think; it was to discipline his parents."

"Well, then, it wasn't fair, mamma. Why should *his* life be taken away for their sake, when he wasn't doing anything?"

"Oh, I don't know! I only know it was for a good and wise and merciful reason."

"What reason, mamma?"

"I think — I think — well, it was a judgment; it was to punish them for some sin they had committed."

"But *he* was the one that was punished, mamma. Was that right?"

"Certainly, certainly. He does nothing that isn't right and wise and merciful. You can't understand these things now, dear, but when you are grown up you will understand them, and then you will see that they are just and wise."

After a pause:

"Did He make the roof fall in on the stranger that was trying to save the crippled old woman from the fire, mamma?"

"Yes, my child. *Wait!* Don't ask me why, because I don't know. I only know it was to discipline someone, or be a judgment upon somebody, or to show His power."

"That drunken man that stuck a pitchfork into Mrs. Welch's baby when —"

"Never mind about it, you needn't go into particulars; it was as to discipline the child — *that* much is certain, anyway."

## Lie Two: God's will is to murder children

If Mr. Twain had loved God and believed his Bible, he wouldn't have made such wild and untrue claims. But he didn't love God. He hated Him, and so a little twisting of Scripture was no doubt justified in his sad and twisted mind.

There are at least two wills of God. There is firstly His *perfect* will. God's will is not what we see on earth. It will eventually be done on earth as it is in heaven, when God's Kingdom comes to this sinful earth. He will then put a stop to the murder of babies with pitchforks, and the murder of babies with sharp scalpels and suction machines, all done in the name of a woman's choice. He will put a stop to rape, hatred, greed, pride, envy, jealousy, adultery, fornication, homosexuality, blasphemy, lust, and a multitude of other things He sees as being evil.

The second will of God is His *permission* will. He *allows* murder in the womb, with a pitchfork, and in Nazi Germany. He allows rape, adultery, theft, lying, blasphemy, lust, fornication, etc. But as each evil is committed, the guilty criminal is storing up His just wrath for his sins (see Romans 2). God, in His great mercy, even allows mockery, blasphemy, and the twisting of Scripture, in the hope that the offender may repent and trust in Jesus — to avoid the damnation of hell.

In Luke 13:1–4 certain people came to Jesus with the same assertions that Mr. Clemens made through Bessie. A number of Galileans had been murdered, and another 18 had died when a tower fell on them:

> Just at that time there [arrived] some people who informed Jesus about the Galileans whose blood Pilate had mixed with their sacrifices. And He replied by saying to them, Do you think that these Galileans were greater sinners than all the other Galileans because they have suffered in this way? I tell you, No; but unless you repent (change your mind for the better and heartily amend your ways, with abhorrence of your past sins), you will all likewise perish *and* be lost eternally. Or those eighteen on whom the tower in Siloam fell and killed them — do you think that they were more guilty offenders (debtors) than all the others who dwelt in Jerusalem? (AMP)

The assertion was that God had judged these unfortunates for their sins. Jesus rebuked them for their presumptions, and told them to rather repent of their own sins. Mr. Twain would have been wise to heed such advice.

"Mamma, Mr. Burgess said in his sermon that billions of little creatures are sent into us to give us cholera, and typhoid, and lockjaw, and more than a thousand other sicknesses and — mamma, does He send them?"

"Oh, certainly, child, certainly. Of course."

"What for?"

"Oh, to discipline us! Haven't I told you so, over and over again?"

"It's awful cruel, mamma! And silly! And if I —"

"Hush, oh *hush!* Do you want to bring the lightning?"

"You know the lightning *did* come last week, mamma, and struck the new church, and burnt it down. Was it to discipline the church?"

(Wearily). "Oh, I suppose so."

"But it killed a hog that wasn't doing anything. Was it to discipline the hog, mamma?"

"Dear child, don't you want to run out and play a while? If you would like to —"

"Mama, only think! Mr. Hollister says there isn't a bird or fish or reptile or any other animal that hasn't got an enemy that Providence has sent to bite it and chase it and pester it, and kill it, and suck its blood and discipline it and make it good and religious. Is that true, mother — because if it is true, why did Mr. Hollister laugh at it?"

"That Hollister is a scandalous person, and I don't want you to listen to anything he says,"

"Why, mamma, he is very interesting, and I think he tries to be good. He says the wasps catch spiders and cram them down into their nests in the ground — *alive*, mamma! — and there they live and suffer days and days and days, and the hungry little wasps chewing their legs and gnawing into their bellies all the time, to make them good and religious and praise God for His infinite mercies. I think Mr.

Hollister is just lovely, and ever so kind; for when I asked him if he would treat a spider like that, he said he hoped to be damned if he would; and then he —"

"My child! oh, do for goodness' sake —"

"And mamma, he says the spider is appointed to catch the fly, and drive her fangs into his bowels, and suck and suck and suck his blood, to discipline him and make him a Christian; and whenever the fly buzzes his wings with the pain and misery of it, you can see by the spider's grateful eye that she is thanking the Giver of All Good for — well, she's saving grace, as he says; and also, he —"

"Oh, aren't you ever going to get tired chattering! If you want to go out and play."

## Lie Three: God created everything as it is

Once again, Mr. Twain completely ignored the Genesis Curse and complained about the plight of the hog, the spider, and the fly. The *whole* of creation: spiders, flies, hogs, frogs, and logs — *everything* is under the Genesis curse. *Nothing* has escaped. The happy, hopping frog eventually croaks and the solid log ultimately rots. The spider eats the fly, and the fly is swatted with the hand. The hand is stung by the bee, and the bee is eaten by the bird. The bird is eaten by the cat, and the dog kills the cat. Dogs would seem therefore to have it made, but they have fleas. The filthy fleas suck their blood; the dog gets sick, gets old, and dies. And so it goes on, and it will go on until God's Kingdom comes to this earth and God's will is done on earth as it is in heaven when the wolf will lie down with the lamb. But Mr. Twain didn't have that glorious hope. All he had was the problem of suffering and death and fleas and flies, for which he blamed the God in whom he didn't believe.

"Mama, he says himself that all troubles and pains and miseries and rotten diseases and horrors and villainies are sent to us in mercy and kindness to discipline us; and he says it is the duty of every father and mother to *help* Providence, every way they can; and says they can't do it by just scolding and whipping, for that won't answer, it is weak and no good — Providence's way is best, and it is every parent's duty and every *person's* duty to help discipline everybody, and cripple them and kill them, and starve them, and freeze them, and rot them with diseases, and lead them into murder and theft and dishonor and disgrace; and he says Providence's invention for disciplining us and the animals is the very brightest idea that ever was, and not even an idiot could get up anything shinier. Mamma, brother Eddie needs disciplining, right away: and I know where you can get the smallpox for him, and the itch, and the diphtheria, and bone-rot, and heart disease, and consumption, and — *Dear* mamma, have you fainted! I will run and bring help! Now *this* comes of staying in town in this hot weather."

## Lie Four: We should cause suffering

Mr. Clemens then builds on his faulty foundation and takes his argument to its logical conclusion. If God wants babies to be thrust through with pitchforks to discipline humanity, we should help Him by killing babies with pitchforks. Once again, keep in mind that his god (the wonderful lofty one who he thinks made all things) is just as guilty as the God he doesn't believe in, who he is blaming for human suffering. God allows suffering, but the Scriptures tell us that it is the god of this world (Satan) who inflicts disease. We see this explained in Scripture through the suffering of Job:

> Now there was a day when the sons of God came to present themselves before the LORD, and Satan also came among them. And the LORD said to Satan, "From where do you come?"
>
> So Satan answered the LORD and said, "From going to and fro on the earth, and from walking back and forth on it."
>
> Then the LORD said to Satan, "Have you considered My servant Job, that there is none like him on the earth, a blameless and upright man, one who fears God and shuns evil?"

So Satan answered the Lord and said, "Does Job fear God for nothing? Have You not made a hedge around him, around his household, and around all that he has on every side? You have blessed the work of his hands, and his possessions have increased in the land. But now, stretch out Your hand and touch all that he has, and he will surely curse You to Your face!"

And the Lord said to Satan, "Behold, all that he has is in your power; only do not lay a hand on his person."

So Satan went out from the presence of the Lord (Job 1:6–12).

This is where Jesus put the blame for human suffering:

But when Jesus saw her, He called her to Him and said to her, "Woman, you are loosed from your infirmity." And He laid His hands on her, and immediately she was made straight, and glorified God.

But the ruler of the synagogue answered with indignation, because Jesus had healed on the Sabbath; and he said to the crowd, "There are six days on which men ought to work; therefore come and be healed on them, and not on the Sabbath day."

The Lord then answered him and said, "Hypocrite! Does not each one of you on the Sabbath loose his ox or donkey from the stall, and lead it away to water it? So ought not this woman, being a daughter of Abraham, whom Satan has bound — think of it — for eighteen years, be loosed from this bond on the Sabbath?" (Luke 13:12–16).

Jesus didn't say that the suffering was God's will because of the woman's karma. He didn't say that God was disciplining her for her sins or trying to make her "good." Instead, He fulfilled the will of God and healed her. This is because the thief came not but to steal, kill, and destroy (see John 10:10). Jesus came to give life and health, not death and suffering.

# CHAPTER SIX

# HE, BEING DEAD, YET SPEAKS

Mark Twain, dead though he is, is speaking volumes to this generation. He is a pied piper who plays a tune that a sinful generation loves to hear. Twain has an unending arsenal of ammunition he passes on to those who want to fight against God and fortify their position that pornography, adultery, fornication, homosexuality, etc., are morally acceptable. This is because if the God of the Bible (the One who requires moral accountability) can be shown to be unjust, He has no case against me for my sins. So in looking closely at Twain's worldview, we are not just looking at a worldview of a dead, bitter man, but one that may be embraced by your nephew, brother, uncle, mother, or sister.

Chapter 2
*Creation of Man*

*Mamma.* You disobedient child, have you been associating with that irreligious Hollister again?

*Bessie.* Well, mamma, he is interesting, anyway, although wicked, and I can't help loving interesting people. Here is the conversation we had:

*Hollister.* Bessie, suppose you should take some meat and bones and fur, and make a cat out of it, and should tell the cat, Now you are not to be unkind to any creature, on pain of punishment and death. And suppose the cat should disobey, and catch a mouse and torture it and kill it. What would you do to the cat?

*Bessie.* Nothing.

*H.* Why?

*B.* Because I know what the cat would say. She would say, It's my nature, I couldn't help it; I didn't make my nature, *you* made it. And so you are responsible for what I've done — I'm not. I couldn't answer that, Mr. Hollister.

*H.* It's just the case of Frankenstein and his Monster over again.

*B.* What is that?

*H.* Frankenstein took some flesh and bones and blood and made a man out of them; the man ran away and fell to raping and robbing and murdering everywhere, and Frankenstein was horrified and in despair, and said, *I* made him, without asking his consent, and it makes me responsible for every crime he commits. *I* am the criminal, he is innocent.

*B.* Of course he was right.

*H.* I judge so. It's just the case of God and man and you and the cat over again.

*B.* How is that?

*H.* God made man, without man's consent, and made his nature, too; made it vicious instead of angelic, and then said, Be angelic, or I will punish you and destroy you. But no matter, God is responsible for everything man does, all the same; He can't get around that fact. There is only one Criminal, and it is not man.

*Mamma.* This is atrocious! It is wicked, blasphemous, irreverent, horrible!

*B.* Yes'm, but it's true. And I'm not going to make a cat. I would be above making a cat if I couldn't make a good one.

**Lie Five: God made man vicious**

The Bible wasn't the reservoir for truth for Mr. Twain to gather information about God. It was rather from other sources, including his fertile imagination. It was Napoleon who said that man will believe anything as long as it's not in the Bible.

The Scriptures tell us that God *didn't* make man "vicious instead of angelic." Neither did He then say, "Be angelic, or I will punish you and destroy you." God made man good, without any sin (see Genesis chapter 1). But instead of believing that, Twain concludes:

> "But no matter, God is responsible for everything man does, all the same; He can't get around that fact. There is only one Criminal, and it is not man."

If Mr. Twain is correct, we should quickly take his evidence to the Supreme Court and make a case for the immediate release of every rapist and murderer from our prisons, because they are *all* innocent. Who would dare waste the court's (and our) time with such a frivolous case? Mark Twain.

Chapter 3

> "Mamma, if a person by the name of Jones kills a person by the name of Smith just for amusement, it's murder, isn't it, and Jones is a murderer?"
> "Yes, my child."
> "And Jones is punishable for it?"
> "Yes, my child."
> "Why, mamma?"

"*Why?* Because God has forbidden homicide in the Ten Commandments, and therefore whoever kills a person commits a crime and must suffer for it."

"But mamma, suppose Jones has by birth such a violent temper that he can't control himself?"

"He *must* control himself. God requires it."

"But he doesn't make his own temper, mamma, he is born with it, like the rabbit and the tiger; and so, why should he be held responsible?"

"Because God *says* he is responsible and *must* control his temper."

"But he can't, mamma; and so, don't you think it is God that does the killing and is responsible, because it was He that gave him the temper which he couldn't control?"

"Peace, my child! He *must* control it, for God requires it, and that ends the matter. It settles it, and there is no room for argument."

(*After a thoughtful pause.*) "It doesn't seem to me to settle it. Mamma, murder is murder, isn't it? And whoever commits it is a murderer? That is the plain simple fact, isn't it?"

(*Suspiciously.*) "What are you arriving at now, my child?"

"Mamma, when God designed Jones He could have given him a rabbit's temper if He had wanted to, couldn't He?"

"Yes."

"Then Jones would not kill anybody and have to be hanged?"

"True."

"But He chose to give Jones a temper that would *make* him kill Smith. Why, then, isn't He responsible?"

"Because He also gave Jones a Bible. The Bible gives Jones ample warning not to commit murder; and so if Jones commits it he alone is responsible."

(*Another pause.*) "Mamma, did God make the house-fly?"

"Certainly, my darling."

"What for?"

"For some great and good purpose, and to display His power."

"What is the great and good purpose, mamma?"

"We do not know, my child. We only know that He makes *all* things for a great and good purpose. But this is too large a subject for a dear little Bessie like you, only a trifle over three years old."

"Possibly, mamma, yet it profoundly interests me. I have been reading about the fly, in the newest science-book. In that book he is called 'the most dangerous animal and the most murderous that exists upon the earth, killing hundreds of thousands of men, women and children every year, by distributing deadly diseases among them.' Think of it, mamma, the *most* fatal of all the animals! By all odds the most murderous of all the living things created by God. Listen to this, from the book:

> Now, the house fly has a very keen scent for filth of any kind. Whenever there is any within a hundred yards or so, the fly goes for it to smear its mouth and all the sticky hairs of its six legs with dirt and disease germs. A second or two suffices to gather up many thousands of these disease germs, and then off goes the fly to the nearest kitchen or dining room. There the fly crawls over the meat, butter, bread, cake, anything it can find, in fact, and often gets into the milk pitcher, depositing large numbers of disease germs at every step. The house fly is as disgusting as it is dangerous.

"Isn't it horrible, mamma! One fly produces fifty-two billions of descendants in 60 days in June and July, and they go and crawl over sick people and wade through pus, and sputa, and foul matter exuding from sores, and gaum themselves with every kind of disease-germ, then they go to everybody's dinner-table and wipe themselves off on the butter and the other food, and many and many a painful illness and ultimate death results from this loathsome industry. Mamma, they murder seven thousand persons in New York City alone, every year — people against whom they have no quarrel. To kill without cause is murder — nobody denies that. Mamma?"

"Well?"

"Have the flies a Bible?"

"Of course not."

"You have said it is the Bible that makes man responsible. If God didn't give him a Bible to circumvent the nature that He deliberately gave him, God would be responsible. He gave the fly his murderous nature, and sent him forth unobstructed by a Bible or any other restraint to commit murder by wholesale. And so, therefore, God is Himself responsible. God is a murderer. Mr. Hollister says so. Mr. Hollister says God can't make one moral law for man and another for Himself. He says it would be laughable."

"Do shut up! I wish that that tiresome Hollister was in Hamburg! He is an ignorant, unreasoning, illogical ass, and I have told you over and over again to keep out of his poisonous company."

### Lie Six: God gave the Bible to show us right from wrong.

Twain accuses God of giving Jones a bad temper and therefore *making* him kill Smith. Let's follow his logic. If God gave a man a lustful heart that desires to commit adultery or rape, it's not the man who is guilty of rape or adultery. It is God because He made him with that nature.

Then Mr. Clemens uses the theologically ignorant Mamma to preach theological ignorance. This way of arguing is commonly known as a "straw man." The person putting forth the argument perpetuates lies and then easily dismantles the lies. He with ease pulls apart the straw man and then pats himself on the back for winning the argument.

Mamma (the straw man/woman) says that Jones is responsible because God gave Him a Bible. Perhaps she was unaware that the printing press was invented by Johannes Gutenberg in 1440, upon which he printed the Gutenberg Bible. Until then, the millions (perhaps billions) didn't have access to the Scriptures, as we know them. Besides, most couldn't read. So how could the Bible make them responsible?

Then there are the millions of heathen who dwelt in the deepest jungles of Africa, the billions of Chinese, Russians, Australians, New Zealanders, etc., who didn't have access to the Scriptures until the last two hundred years. If murderous Jones was responsible because God gave him a Bible, then the billions down through the ages who didn't have a Bible *cannot* be held guilty. They sinned in complete ignorance.

However, Romans chapters 1 and 2 tell us that God has given every son and daughter of Adam the powerful restraint of a conscience (*con* means "with" and *science* means "knowledge"). It's there for the angry man who doesn't have the temperament of a rabbit. It's there for the lustful man who burns with a desire to rape, fornicate, commit adultery, or drink in pornographic images. The conscience was given by God, is shaped by society, and is universal. The Russians, the Chinese, the tribes of deep Africa, and Mark Twain (as well and you and I) were all given the impartial judge in the courtroom of the mind. It's up to us whether or not we listen to that voice.

Chapter 4

> "Mamma, what is a virgin?"
>
> "A maid."
>
> "Well, what is a maid?"
>
> "A girl or woman that isn't married."
>
> "Uncle Jonas says that sometimes a virgin that has been having a child —"
>
> "Nonsense! A virgin can't have a child."
>
> "Why can't she, mamma?"
>
> "Well, there are reasons why she can't."
>
> "What reasons, mamma?"
>
> "Physiological. She would have to cease to be a virgin before she could have the child."

"How do you mean, mamma?"

"Well, let me see. It's something like this: a Jew couldn't be a Jew after he had become a Christian; he couldn't be Christian and Jew at the same time. Very well, a person couldn't be mother and virgin at the same time."

"Why, mamma, Sally Brooks has had a child, and *she's* a virgin."

"Indeed? Who says so?"

"She says so herself."

"Oh. No doubt! Are there any other witnesses?"

"Yes — there's a dream. She says the governor's private secretary appeared to her in a dream and told her she was going to have a child, and it came out just so."

"I shouldn't wonder! Did he say the governor was the correspondent?"

### Lie Seven: A Jew cannot be a Christian, therefore Mary wasn't a virgin

It seems that Mr. Clemens did believe some portions of Scripture. Mary did have at least five more children after she had Jesus, so she was no longer a virgin after she bore Jesus:

> Then He went out from there and came to His own country, and His disciples followed Him. And when the Sabbath had come, He began to teach in the synagogue. And many hearing Him were astonished, saying, "Where did this Man get these things? And what wisdom is this which is given to Him, that such mighty works are performed by His hands! Is this not the carpenter, the Son of Mary, and brother of James, Joses, Judas, and Simon? And are not His sisters here with us?" So they were offended at Him (Mark 6:1–3).

Then Clemens said, "Well, let me see. It's something like this: a Jew couldn't be a Jew after he had become a Christian; he couldn't be Christian and Jew at the same time. Very well, a person couldn't be mother and virgin at the same time." I was born with Jewish blood, and when I became a Christian I kept my Jewish blood. I'm not alone. *All* of the disciples were Jewish and they were Christians. So were the 3,000 Jews who were converted on the day of Pentecost when the first sermon was preached. Twain's "Very well" is unfounded. He was wrong about a Jew not being a Christian, and he was wrong about Mary being a virgin and being the mother of Jesus.

Chapter 5

"Mamma, didn't you tell me an ex-governor, like Mr. Burlap, is a person that's been governor but isn't a governor anymore?"

"Yes, dear."

"And Mr. Williams said 'ex' always stands for a Has Been, didn't he?"

"Yes, child. It is a vulgar way of putting it, but it expresses the fact."

(Eagerly). "So then Mr. Hollister was right, after all. He says the Virgin Mary isn't a virgin any more, she's a Has Been. He says. . . ."

"It is false! Oh, it was just like that godless miscreant to try to undermine an innocent child's holy belief with his foolish lies; and if I could have my way, I. . . ."

"But mama — honest and true — *is* she still a virgin — a *real* virgin, you know?"

"Certainly she is; and has never been anything *but* a virgin — oh, the adorable One, the pure, the spotless, the undefiled!"

"Why, mama, Mr. Hollister says she *can't* be. That's what *he* says. He says she had five children after she had the One that was begotten by absent treatment and didn't break anything and he thinks such a lot of child-bearing, spread over years and years and years, would ultimately wear a virgin's virginity so thin that even Wall street would consider the stock too lavishly watered and you couldn't place it there at any discount you could name, because the

Board would say it was wildcat, and wouldn't list it. That's what *he* says. And besides. . . ."

"Go to the nursery, instantly! Go!"

## Lie Eight: Roman Catholicism and biblical Christianity are synonymous

Mr. Twain finally reveals that Mamma is a Roman Catholic. She says of Mary's virginity, "Certainly she is; and has never been anything *but* a virgin — oh, the adorable One, the pure, the spotless, the undefiled!" A Roman Catholic believes in the sinless nature of Mary. A Protestant who knows his Bible will protest and say that she was blessed to carry Jesus, but she was a sinner like the rest of humanity. This is because the Bible says, "All have sinned" (Romans 3:23). It also says "There is none righteous, no, not one" (Romans 3:10). Mary said that she needed a Savior (see Luke 1:47). Only sinners need a Savior. She was also present on the Day of Pentecost where she received the Holy Spirit and had her sins washed away. Roman Catholics who have truly repented, trusted alone in Jesus, and have been born again are Christians, but the Roman Catholic religion at its core is not the same as biblical Christianity. It is Roman Catholic, having its own set of beliefs and dogmas and its own Bible.

Chapter 6

"Mamma, is Christ God?"

"Yes, my child."

"Mamma, how can He be Himself and Somebody Else at the same time?"

"He isn't, my darling. It is like the Siamese twins — two persons, one born ahead of the other, but equal in authority, equal in power."

"I understand it, now, mamma, and it is quite simple. One twin has sexual intercourse with his mother, and begets himself and his brother; and next he has sexual intercourse with his grandmother and begets his mother. I should think it would be difficult, mamma, though interesting. Oh, ever so difficult. I should think that the Correspondent —"

"All things are possible with God, my child."

"Yes, I suppose so. But not with another Siamese twin, I suppose. *You* don't think any ordinary Siamese twin could beget himself and his brother on his mother, do you, mamma, and then go on back while his hand is in and beget *her*, too, on his grandmother?"

"Certainly not, my child. None but God can do these wonderful and holy miracles."

"And enjoy them. For of course He enjoys them, or He wouldn't go foraging around among the family like that, would He, mamma? — injuring their reputations in the village and causing talk. Mr. Hollister says it was wonderful and awe-inspiring in those days, but wouldn't work now. He says that if the Virgin lived in Chicago now, and got in the family way and explained to the newspaper fellows that God was the Correspondent, she couldn't get two in ten of them to believe it. He says there are a h-ll of a lot!"

"My child!"

"Well, that is what he says, anyway."

"Oh, I do *wish* you would keep away from that wicked, wicked man!"

"He doesn't *mean* to be wicked, mamma, and he doesn't blame God. No, he doesn't blame Him; he says they all do it — gods do. It's their habit, they've always been that way."

"What way, dear?"

"Going around unvirgining the virgins. He says our God did not invent the idea — it was old and mouldy before He happened on it. Says He hasn't invented anything, but got His Bible and His Flood and His morals and all His ideas from earlier gods, and they got them from still earlier gods. He says there never was a god yet that wasn't born of a Virgin. Mr. Hollister says no virgin is safe where a god is. He says he wishes he was a god; he says he would make virgins so scarce that. . . ."

"Peace, peace! *Don't* run on so, my child. If you. . . ."

". . . and he advised me to lock my door nights, because. . . ."

"Hush, hush, will you!"

". . . because although I am only three and a half years old and quite safe from men. . . ."

"Mary Ann, come and get this child! There, now, go along with you, and don't come near me again until you can interest yourself in some subject of a lower grade and less awful than theology. . . ."

Bessie, (disappearing.) "Mr. Hollister says there *ain't* any."

## Lie Nine: That God and Jesus are like Siamese twins

Bessie asked, "Mamma, is Christ God?" and followed with "Mamma, how can He be Himself and Somebody Else at the same time?" This was Mamma's opportunity to expound Holy Scripture. Instead, she gives a dimwitted analogy about Siamese twins which gives Twain opportunity to talk about his favorite subject and blaspheme God at the same time. The Bible says:

And without controversy great is the mystery of godliness:

> God was manifest in the flesh,
> Justified in the Spirit,
> Seen of angels,
> Preached unto the Gentiles,
> Believed on in the world,
> Received up into glory (1 Timothy 3:16; KJV).

When Almighty God (the upholder of the universe) created a body in Jesus of Nazareth, He didn't cease to be Almighty God. He still upheld the universe. Jesus was the express image of the invisible God. It is so simple a three-year-old child could understand it. But Twain's Bessie was no ordinary three-year-old. She wasn't just a student of philosophy and biblical theology; she was also well versed in the birds and the bees and the perversion of incest.

Samuel Clemens hid himself behind the name of Mark Twain, and then distanced himself further behind a non-existent little girl.

His biblically twisted and sexually perverted childish scenario was written in an effort to mock and discredit the character of God so that he could justify his sins. No wonder he wanted it published when he was dead. It certainly would have been considered sexually perverted and blasphemous in his day. However, the tragedy is that he mistakenly thought that after 100 years, the grave would surely save him from the consequences of such idle words. But there is going to be a resurrection of the just and the unjust, and Jesus warned:

> "But I say to you that for every idle word men may speak, they will give account of it in the day of judgment" (Matthew 12:36).

# CHAPTER SEVEN

# GOD'S UNFAIR SEXUAL DISPERSION

In Letter VIII of *Letters from the Earth,* Mr. Twain bemoans the fact that the Ten Commandments forbid adultery. In the book, he writes on behalf of his spiritual father (Satan) words that come naturally to his children.

Satan visits the earth and writes letters to the Archangel's Michael and Gabriel, regarding his thoughts about humanity and their beliefs. This gives him an opportunity to mock God and heaven, saying that it's a place filled with things that we don't value.

His little twist is that he doesn't call sin "sin," but the "Law of Nature," saying that God gave us natural desires, but that He then gave us the Law of God which forbids the following of those desires. Therefore, God is guilty of sin, and you and I are blameless, innocent, and we are to be pitied rather than judged.

It's interesting to note that he doesn't address the Commandments that forbid stealing and murder. If God is the criminal, then thieves and murderers are innocent and He is the one who is guilty. Twain's philosophy only works when it comes to sexual inclinations.

He then quotes the Seventh Commandment saying that it makes no age distinction:

> "Thou shalt not commit adultery" is a command which makes no distinction between the following persons. They are all required to obey it: Children at birth. Children in the cradle. School children. Youths and maidens. Fresh adults. Older ones. Men and women of 40. Of 50. Of 60. Of 70. Of 80. Of 90. Of 100. The command does not distribute its burden equally, and cannot. It is not hard upon the three sets of children. It is hard — harder — still harder upon the next three sets — cruelly hard. It is blessedly softened to the next three sets.[1]

He is saying that the Law is most restrictive upon those we refer to as having raging hormones. Sexual sin is most tempting for "youths" and "fresh adults." So God is unfair to restrict sexual activity at the age that it's most desired. He wants to let the hungry dog off the leash to satisfy its God-given appetite. King Solomon speaks instead of restraint. When speaking to his son he *warns* against sexual sin:

> My son, pay attention to my wisdom; lend your ear to my understanding, that you may preserve discretion, and your lips may keep knowledge. For the lips of an immoral woman drip honey, and her mouth is smoother than oil; but in the end she is bitter as wormwood, sharp as a two-edged sword. Her feet go down to death, her steps lay hold of hell. . . . Let your fountain be blessed, and rejoice with the wife of your youth. As a loving deer and a graceful doe, let her breasts satisfy you at all times; and always be enraptured with her love. For why should

---

1. Twain, *Letters from the Earth*, "Letter VIII."

you, my son, be enraptured by an immoral woman, and be embraced in the arms of a seductress? For the ways of man are before the eyes of the LORD, and He ponders all his paths (Proverbs 5:1–5, 18–21).

If a man doesn't fear God, he will naturally have eyes that are "full of adultery."[2] He will burn with lust, and look for opportunity to put out the raging fire. But Solomon was wise. He knew that it is the fear of God that keeps a man from committing adultery, or even *imagining* it through lust. He knew that the ways of man are "before the eyes of the Lord" and God will hold us accountable. This was Joseph's experience when Potiphar's wife tried to entice him into adultery:

> And it came to pass after these things that his master's wife cast longing eyes on Joseph, and she said, "Lie with me."
> But he refused and said to his master's wife, "Look, my master does not know what is with me in the house, and he has committed all that he has to my hand. There is no one greater in this house than I, nor has he kept back anything from me but you, because you are his wife. How then can I do this great wickedness, and sin against God?"
> So it was, as she spoke to Joseph day by day, that he did not heed her, to lie with her or to be with her.
> But it happened about this time, when Joseph went into the house to do his work, and none of the men of the house was inside, that she caught him by his garment, saying, "Lie with me." But he left his garment in her hand, and fled and ran outside (Genesis 39:7–12).

Notice Joseph's reasons for refusing such enticing pleasure. He was firstly concerned about a betrayal of his master's trust, and secondly (and more importantly) he was concerned about God's disapproval of his actions. He asked, "How then can I do this great wickedness, *and* sin against God?"

---

2. See 2 Peter 2:14.

Joseph believed that disloyalty to Potiphar was a "great wickedness." Adultery not only violates the Seventh Commandment, but it violates the Tenth through covetousness, and the First because when we sin against another human being we are failing to love our neighbor as much as we love ourselves:

> For the commandments, "You shall not commit adultery," "You shall not murder," "You shall not steal," "You shall not bear false witness," "You shall not covet," and if there is any other commandment, are all summed up in this saying, namely, "You shall love your neighbor as yourself" (Romans 13:9).

So when Joseph talked about sinning against God, there was the dual sin of betrayal of trust *and* the sin of adultery. If he had no fear of God, neither would have been considered a sin, and no doubt Joseph would have yielded to the temptation — as do millions who have no understanding of God or of His power to cast body and soul into hell.[3]

Joseph was a "type" of Christ. He was unique among men. If you study his amazing life you will see that he was, like Jesus, incredibly gracious and forgiving toward those who wronged him. He was able to resist bitterness, resentment, and hatred, and he was able to resist sexual sin as we see with Potiphar's lusty wife.

When the Apostle Paul spoke of those who wouldn't enter the Kingdom of God, he didn't leave out fornicators or adulterers. He firstly told his hearers not to be deceived, and listed those who won't make it to heaven:

> Neither fornicators, nor idolaters, nor adulterers, nor homosexuals, nor sodomites, nor thieves, nor covetous, nor drunkards, nor revilers, nor extortioners will inherit the kingdom of God (1 Corinthians 6:9–10).

But in the next verse he says "and such were some of you." Christians are no strangers to adultery, lust-filled thoughts, homosexuality,

---

3. See Matthew 10:28.

lying, and stealing. We are *all* sinners, and yet God is merciful to forgive all who repent and trust in Jesus. The miracle is that He not only forgives us, but He gives us His Holy Spirit to help us resist what would normally be overwhelming temptations that come at us like a steamroller over tiny ants.

**Twain's Trained Eye**

No doubt, Mark Twain could see sexual sin in others because he could see it in himself. He was a normal red-blooded male who couldn't help himself when he felt the power of sin within his own heart. This is why he could confidently say (when speaking of the elderly and sexual desire):

> It has now done all the damage it can, and might as well be put out of commission. Yet with comical imbecility it is continued, and the four remaining estates are put under its crushing ban. Poor old wrecks, they couldn't disobey if they tried. And think — because they holily refrain from adulterating each other, they get praise for it! Which is nonsense; for even the Bible knows enough to know that if the oldest veteran there could get his lost heyday back again for an hour he would cast that commandment to the winds and ruin the first woman he came across, even though she were an entire stranger.[4]

It's ironic that Twain saw that the battle was with the Law of God, because 1,900 years earlier, the Apostle Paul spoke of the same battle. He too saw the conflict between what he wanted to do, and how the Law of God forbad this insatiable desire to follow what Twain saw as "the Law of nature" — what the Bibles reveals is a carnal inclination to violate the Law of God:

> I find then a law, that evil is present with me, the one who wills to do good. For I delight in the law of God according to the inward man. But I see another law in my members, warring against the law of my mind, and bringing

---

4. Twain, *Letters from the Earth*, "Letter VIII."

me into captivity to the law of sin which is in my members. O wretched man that I am! Who will deliver me from this body of death? I thank God — through Jesus Christ our Lord! So then, with the mind I myself serve the law of God, but with the flesh the law of sin (Romans 7:21–27).

Twain faults the Law because he doesn't understand its purpose. Keep in mind that when the Tenth Commandment says "Thou shalt not covet," it includes lusting after your neighbor's wife (see Exodus 20:17). This is what Scripture says about the purpose of the moral Law (the Ten Commandments):

What shall we say then? Is the law sin? Certainly not! On the contrary, I would not have known sin except through the law. For I would not have known covetousness unless the law had said, "You shall not covet" (Romans 7:7).

The Law was given as a mirror to show Paul his sin of lust. It reflected his true moral state. When he said that he hadn't *known* lust unless the Law had forbidden it, he was saying that he didn't see lust in truth — as a sin against God.

When I saw my personal transgressions for the first time back on a dark night in April 1972, I was sickened — not because I had sinned, *but because I so loved and lived for the sin that was being condemned.* Lust meant instant pleasure in a world that tended to be dull and boring. I had to work at finding pleasure through sport, through parties, etc., but lust was *instantaneous* and never ending. It was gratifying, easy, and a continual source of joy. I enjoyed lust.

So the first inclination we have when confronted by God's Law is to have a shoot-out — we resist arrest and fight to keep the precious contraband. Thus, we become hostile to the Law. This is why Paul asks the question "Is the Law sin?" Is it right in its accusation? To which he replies, "God forbid." The fault is not with the Law. The fault is with the criminals.

Mark Twain heard the Law saying that his desires were unclean, and consequentially became angry with the mirror, when all it was doing was reflecting the truth.

Paul goes on to say that the Law is holy, just, and good. There's nothing wrong with the reflection. It's a *good* mirror. The problem is that each of us is morally unclean, and contrary to popular belief, the mirror can't help us. That's not its purpose. No one in their right mind tries to wash themselves with a mirror. It just makes us aware that we need cleansing. It helps us to understand our guilt before a morally perfect God, and thus the need for His mercy. But look at how an angry Twain turns his rage and frustration on the mirror-Giver:

> These people's God has shown them by a million acts that He respects none of the Bible's statutes. He breaks every one of them himself, adultery and all.[5]

There are a number of factors that take a sin-loving sinner from being angry at the Law to conversion. Of course, every person who is converted to Jesus Christ is converted by the grace of God. We are saved by grace through faith (see Ephesians 2:8–9). However, it's the Law of God that brings "the knowledge of sin" (see Romans 7:7 and 7:13) and shows us that we need God's amazing grace.

Imagine if I gave you a tall glass of cool, clear water on a hot day. You are very thirsty so you immediately pick it up and put it to your dry and longing lips. But I then say that the water contains a drop of arsenic. That knowledge changes everything. It leaves you with a choice. If you believe the information given to you, your thirst will become secondary. If you don't believe it, you will drink it and die in agony.

The Law brings the knowledge of sin and shows us that sin is "exceedingly sinful." The night of my conversion I simply believed what I heard, realized that I had greatly offended a morally perfect God, and had incurred His just wrath (see John 3:36). I was His enemy in the same way a devious murder is the enemy of a good judge. Those who have that understanding no longer drink iniquity like water.

---

5. Ibid.

# CHAPTER EIGHT

# WITCHES, BABIES, AND HELL

There are no witches. The witch text remains; only the practice has changed. Hell fire is gone, but the text remains. Infant damnation is gone, but the text remains. More than two hundred death penalties are gone from the law books, but the texts that authorized them remain.[1]

While most of us believe that there are no witches flying across the skies on broomsticks, despite Mr. Twain's denial of their existence, there certainly are genuine witches, both in the Bible, in history, and in contemporary society. The dictionary tells us that a witch is:

---

1. Mark Twain, *Europe and Elsewhere*, "Bible Teaching and Religious Practice" (New York: Harper & Brothers, 1923), p. 387, quoted inHarnesberger, *Mark Twain at Your Fingertips*.

A person, especially a woman, who professes or is supposed to practice magic, especially black magic or the black art; sorceress.

A witch is someone who delves into the demonic realm, a practice forbidden and punishable by death in the Old Testament:

You shall not permit a sorceress to live. (Exodus 22:18). There shall not be found among you anyone who makes his son or his daughter pass through the fire, or one who practices witchcraft, or a soothsayer, or one who interprets omens, or a sorcerer (Deuteronomy 18:10).

*Time* magazine said,

It may be surprising to learn there were witches in biblical times. But according to 1 Samuel, Saul (the first King of Israel) was concerned about the outcome of his tribe's impending battle against the Philistines. So even though sorcery was outlawed in his kingdom, Saul disguised himself and sought the services of a woman at Endor to conjure up the spirit of Samuel (a leader of ancient Israel), who informed him that he and his sons would die the next day in combat.[2]

We know that witches exist, and we also know that the biblical text does remain. This doesn't mean that we should execute fortune-tellers and those who practice witchcraft. Why does Mark Twain think that we should instigate 3,000-year-old Hebrew law? We have laws for our own country, and witches have a right to practice their religion in the United States — a right protected by the Constitution, in the Bill of Rights.

In 1985, Dettmer v Landon (617 F Supp 592) the District Court of Virginia pursuant to rule 52 (a) of the Federal Rules of Civil Procedure ruled that Witchcraft is a legitimate religion and falls within a recognizable religious

---

2. Josh Sanburn, "The Witch of Endor," *Time Magazine*, September 21, 2010, www.time.com/time/specials/packages/article/0,28804,2020423 _2020422_2020430,00.html.

category. In 1986 in the Federal Appeals court fourth circuit, Butzner, J. affirmed the decision (799 F 2d 929). Since in most cases Federal law, even case law supersedes state law in this type of matter, the affirmation by judge Butzner clearly sets Witchcraft as a religion under the protection of constitutional rights.[3]

After mistakenly stating that there were no witches, Mark Twain continues by saying, "Hell fire is gone, but the text remains." I'm not sure where he obtained his information about either hell having no fire, or hell not existing, but he is mistaken once again. I, too, would like to believe that hell doesn't exist, but I know that its reality isn't determined by my belief or non-belief in its existence. If someone who had never visited New York didn't believe that it existed as a city, I could show them pictures and video of its high-risers, but hell has even more compelling evidence for its actuality. C.S. Lewis was right when he said, "There is no doctrine which I would more willingly remove from Christianity than the doctrine of hell, if it lay in my power. But it has the full support of Scripture and, especially, of our Lord's own words; it has always been held by the Christian Church, and it has the support of reason."[4]

There are many Scriptures that make reference to hell as a real place. Here are just four:

The wicked shall be turned into hell, and all the nations that forget God (Psalm 9:17).

If your right eye causes you to sin, pluck it out and cast it from you; for it is more profitable for you that one of your members perish, than for your whole body to be cast into hell. And if your right hand causes you to sin, cut it off and cast it from you; for it is more profitable for you that one of your members perish, than for your whole body to be cast into hell (Matthew 5:29–30).

---

3. "Your Rights and the Law," Pagan and Proud of It, www.paganandproudofit.com/Witchcraft-and-the-law.html.
4. C.S. Lewis, *The Problem of Pain* (New York, NY: HarperOne, 2001), chapter 8.

> And if thy foot offend thee, cut it off: it is better for thee to enter halt into life, than having two feet to be cast into hell, into the fire that never shall be quenched: Where their worm dieth not, and the fire is not quenched (Mark 9:45–46; KJV).

> But I will forewarn you whom ye shall fear: Fear him, which after he hath killed hath power to cast into hell; yea, I say unto you, Fear him (Luke 12:5; KJV).

The Bible is called the "book of law" 18 times in the Old Testament and once in the new (see Galatians 3:10). This is because it expounds both man's law (for the Hebrew nation) and God's Law (for the human race — see Romans 3:19–20). Its credibility isn't dependent on our acceptance of it as such, just as civil law isn't dependent upon the criminal world's acceptance. Its authority has nothing to do with the criminal.

If we violate man's law and are caught, we suffer the consequences. If we violate God's Law (and all of us are caught in our transgressions) we will suffer the consequences, despite unbelief. The Bible warns, "Though they join forces, the wicked will not go unpunished" (Proverbs 11:21). Even if all of humanity agreed with Mark Twain that hell's fire has gone, it certainly remains in Scripture and in reality. God will punish evil.

Those who think that believing the Bible necessitates blind faith need only study its prophecies. This proves that it is indeed the Word of God, and therefore its threatenings of justice will be fulfilled.

## The Support of Reason

Earlier in this book we looked at an incident where Native American Indians committed unspeakably atrocities on an innocent family. If they had been tried in a court of law, what sort of judge would see undeniable evidence of the crimes and have simply dismissed the case? It seems that the indignant Mr. Twain's god would do just that. He would let those cruel murders go without any justice. It is *his* god who is as bad as the murderers. In contrast, the God of creation revealed in the Bible is nothing like Twain's dumb unthinking and unspeaking idol. The Scriptures call Him "the Habitation of Justice," and He will see to it that justice is done on Judgment Day. The belief that if God is good He must punish evil is simple common sense and lines up with the power of reason.

Twain said, "Good friends, good books and a sleepy conscience: this is the ideal."[5] It is good advice indeed to have good friends and good books, but to instruct to have a sleepy conscience is a philosophy for criminals. It is the ideal for fools.

An old drunk once stumbled along a sidewalk heading for his home. His faithful dog saw him approaching and watched his every move. As he entered his home, his dog joyfully followed him. When the drunken man collapsed on the floor in his living room, the dog snuggled up to him, waiting for his master to wake up.

Suddenly, in the middle of the night, the old drunk was roused by the dog's barking. The last thing he wanted was a barking dog! He staggered to his feet, grabbed a chair and threw it at the dog, then collapsed again.

It the morning he awoke to a shocking sight. Thieves had broken into the house in the night and stolen everything he owned — everything, that is, except a broken chair and a dead dog. His faithful friend had been trying to warn him of danger and he had killed the best friend he had.

God gave you a best friend. It's your conscience. Conscience therefore should be treated with the utmost respect. To ignore its voice of warning is to treat it like an enemy. His twisted advice should rather have been "Good friends, the Good Book, and a conscience that is awake and doing its duty: this is the ideal."

His words reveal his love for that which the conscience exposes and condemns — lying, theft, blasphemy, fornication, lust, adultery, godlessness, and all the other vices the human heart so joyfully embraces. Any talk about having a primed and alert conscience flies in the face of this godless world. This is because they don't see sin as an enemy, but as a beloved friend. They embrace it, and they mock those who fight against it. However, on Judgment Day, that friend

---

5. *Mark Twain's Notebook*, 1935, p. 347. Quoted in Harnesberger, *Mark Twain at Your Fingertips*

will prove to be a deadly Judas, and those who fall under its deception will see that guilt-free sin is a delusion.

## More Twain Lies

Those who look for an excuse to enjoy the pleasures of sin tend to believe anything negative about the Bible. If we don't like a particular person and we hear something negative about them we are more likely to embrace it and believe it rather than something negative we hear about someone we love. This is because more negativity fortifies and justifies what we already believe and there is no incentive to search out the truth. Look at what Scripture says about the ungodly who embrace a lie rather than receive the truth:

> And with all unrighteous deception among those who perish, because they did not receive the love of the truth, that they might be saved. And for this reason God will send them strong delusion, that they should believe the lie, that they all may be condemned who did not believe the truth but had pleasure in unrighteousness (2 Thessalonians 2:10-12).

Bearing in mind that all of God's judgments are "true and righteous altogether" (Psalm 19:9), God gives those who love lies over to a strong delusion. Such it seems was the case with Mark Twain. He also said, "Infant damnation is gone, but the text remains." If you do an Internet search of "Infant damnation is gone, but the text remains" you will find that the words have spread like wildfire on bone-dry volatile atheist websites. Christopher Hitchens quotes the words in his book *The Portable Atheist: Essential Readings for the Nonbeliever*[6] with no questioning of the truth of the source.

But here's the problem when the source isn't given — what is the "text" to which he is referring? There are 31,102 verses in the King James Version Bible, and to disprove his statement, we need to know every verse. I have been reading the Scriptures daily for more than 40 years and know of no text that says that infants are damned.

---

6. Christopher Hitchens, *The Portable Atheist: Essential Readings for the Nonbeliever* (Philadelphia, PA: Da Capo Press, 2007), p. 122.

Rather, I have found the opposite. Was Mr. Twain not familiar with the famous words of Scripture: "But when Jesus saw it, He was greatly displeased and said to them, 'Let the little children come to Me, and do not forbid them; for of such is the kingdom of God' " (Mark 10:14)?

When King David's baby died, he had assurance of the child's salvation rather than his damnation. Why would God hold babies accountable for their sins? What "sins" does an infant commit? Does he or she lie, steal, lust, or commit adultery? Does the baby covet or make a god in his own image? The Scriptures tell us that sin is transgression of God's Law (the Ten Commandments — 1 John 3:4) and an infant is incapable of violating that Law. So Mark Twain has either twisted a Bible verse to say something it doesn't mean, he was confused or mistaken, or he was lying. Whatever the case, he has perpetrated a lie that has been embraced and passed on as the truth, and this has caused many to be wrongly offended by the Bible and the gospel that offers them everlasting life. And if they have embraced the lie because they reject the truth, like Twain, they will have a strong delusion.

Sadly, it's human nature to believe and pass on rumors that have no basis in truth. Take for example the rumor that Hasidim Jews are so religiously narrow-minded that they consummate their marriage through a hole in a sheet. I had heard that and couldn't believe that any human being could be so narrow-minded to a point of insanity. No wonder people persecute the Jews when they insist on such insanity. However, when Hasidim Jews were asked if it was true, here is the response:[7]

> NO! According to urban legend, this silly rumor got started in the ghettos of Europe, where some people saw the four-cornered garments with fringes (which do have a hole in the middle for the head) hanging on the wash line.[8] They didn't know what they were for, so their imaginations took over. . . . Hasidism — and Judaism in general — regard

7. Experts123, www.experts123.com/q/do-hasidim-really-have-sex-through-a-hole-in-a-sheet.html.
8. See http://www.snopes.com/religion/sheet.htm.

sex as a natural and beautiful thing, so long as it remains between spouses in privacy. The fact that Hasidim tend to have a lot of children should tell you that we have nothing against sex! We do, however, object to seeing intimate moments and bare bodies in movies and billboards, because we feel it cheapens something that is sacred and private. I suppose this is also the place to dispel the urban legend about how Hasidim supposedly display the bloody sheets on the morning after the wedding night to prove the bride was a virgin. No, we don't do that one, either.

Those who seek the truth go to the source.

# CHAPTER NINE

# THE SEXUALITY OF THE GOAT AND TORTOISE

The fault-finding Mr. Twain not only found fault with God but found fault in all of humanity. He could see sin in everyone but himself. Such is the way of the deceit of conceit. It puts a log in the eye and blinds us to our own sins.

He said,

> I suspect that to you there is still dignity in human life, and that Man is not a joke — a poor joke — the poorest that was ever contrived — an April-fool joke, played by a malicious Creator with nothing better to waste his time upon. . . . Man is not to me the respect-worthy person he was before; and so I have lost my pride in him and can't

write gaily nor praisefully about him anymore. And I don't intend to try.[1]

Using Satan to mask his mockery, he specifically points his finger at those who have faith in God:

> Moreover — if I may put another strain upon you — he thinks he is the Creator's pet. He believes the Creator is proud of him; he even believes the Creator loves him; has a passion for him; sits up nights to admire him; yes, and watch over him and keep him out of trouble. He prays to Him, and thinks He listens. Isn't it a quaint idea? Fills his prayers with crude and bald and florid flatteries of Him, and thinks He sits and purrs over these extravagancies and enjoys them. He prays for help, and favor, and protection, every day; and does it with hopefulness and confidence, too, although no prayer of his has ever been answered. The daily affront, the daily defeat, do not discourage him, he goes on praying just the same. There is something almost fine about this perseverance. I must put one more strain upon you: he thinks he is going to heaven! He has salaried teachers who tell him that. They also tell him there is a hell, of everlasting fire, and that he will go to it if he doesn't keep the Commandments. What are Commandments? They are a curiosity. I will tell you about them by and by.[2]

Here he touches on legitimate Christian doctrine. He speaks of God's love for humanity, His preserving hand, His ear being open to our prayers, our persistence in prayer, and our assurance of salvation. However, these doctrines don't find their source in salaried teachers but in the Word of God. What a tragedy that a man can know so much and yet miss the forest of everlasting life because of the trees of pride. Had Twain humbled himself and sought truth

---

1. James Melville Cox, *Mark Twain: The Fate of Humor*, Letter to William Dean Howells, April 2, 1899 (University of Missouri Press, ), p. 288.
2. *Letters From The Earth* by Mark Twain, http://www.classicreader.com/book/1930/2/.

rather than sin he would have had the veil removed from his eyes. God's love is expressed in the Cross of Jesus Christ. It is there that the light shines in the darkness. But if a man is proud he will never let the Commandments stir his conscience, bring the knowledge of sin, and usher in the revelation that Christ died for us while we were yet sinners.

And so the Commandments, which should have showed him his sin and driven him to the Savior, just condemned him. The Law of God pointed its finger and demanded his death sentence. This is in contrast to the Law for the Christian whose sins are washed away by the grace of God. He says with David, "Oh how I love your Law. It is my mediation night and day," or with the Apostle Paul, "I delight in the Law of God." We are no longer law-breakers, running from the Law. So Twain's carnal mind stayed in a state of hostility toward God — specifically His moral Law (see Romans 8:7).

Look at this interesting attempt to try and shake off guilt the Law brings by blaming God for the sins of men:

> The Bible and man's statutes forbid murder, adultery, fornication, lying, treachery, robbery, oppression and other crimes, but contend that God is free of these laws and has a right to break them when he will. He concedes that God gives to each man his temperament, his disposition, at birth; he concedes that man cannot by any process change this temperament, but must remain always under its dominion. Yet if it be full of dreadful passions, in one man's case, and barren of them in another man's, it is right and rational to punish the one for his crimes, and reward the other for abstaining from crime.
>
> There — let us consider these curiosities. Take two extremes of temperament — the goat and the tortoise. Neither of these creatures makes its own temperament, but is born with it, like man, and can no more change it than can man. Temperament is the law of God written in the heart of every creature by God's own hand, and *must* be obeyed,

and will be obeyed in spite of all restricting or forbidding statutes, let them emanate whence they may.

Very well, lust is the dominant feature of the goat's temperament, the law of God is in its heart, and it must obey it and *will* obey it the whole day long in the rutting season, without stopping to eat or drink. If the Bible said to the goat, "Thou shalt not fornicate, thou shalt not commit adultery," even Man — sap-headed man — would recognize the foolishness of the prohibition, and would grant that the goat ought not to be punished for obeying the law of his Maker. Yet he thinks it right and just that man should be put under the prohibition. All men. All alike.

On its face this is stupid, for, by temperament, which is the *real law* of God, many men are goats and can't help committing adultery when they get a chance; whereas there are numbers of men who, by temperament, can keep their purity and let an opportunity go by if the woman lacks in attractiveness. But the Bible doesn't allow adultery at all, whether a person can help it or not.[3]

This is sad and even pathetic. Think of what this normally brilliant man is saying: "The Bible doesn't allow adultery at all, whether a person can help it or not." Who is this "man" of whom he is speaking? Adultery is the willful and sinful act of taking another man's wife. No man is in a state where he cannot help it; no more than a man cannot help but rob a bank. He is taking something that belongs to another person. But to try and justify adultery, Twain uses the goat who cannot help but take another goat's wife. Such is the extreme men will go to, to try and justify their sin.

It allows no distinction between goat and tortoise — the excitable goat, the emotional goat, that has to have some adultery every day or fade and die; and the tortoise, that cold calm puritan, that takes a treat only once in two years and then goes to sleep in the midst of it and doesn't

3. http://www.classicreader.com/book/1930/9/.

wake up for sixty days. No lady goat is safe from criminal assault, even on the Sabbath Day, when there is a gentleman goat within three miles to leeward of her and nothing in the way but a fence fourteen feet high, whereas neither the gentleman tortoise nor the lady tortoise is ever hungry enough for solemn joys of fornication to be willing to break the Sabbath to get them. Now according to man's curious reasoning, the goat has earned punishment, and the tortoise praise.[4]

Mark Twain would have loved living in contemporary society. In his day he merely whined about the unfairness of God in making the goat sexually hot and the tortoise slow on the uptake. Had he been alive today he could have become a believer in Darwinian evolution, and hiding behind the skirts of science he could have confidently said that man is an animal and therefore sexual sin isn't sin but a mere instinct. Had he lived today he could have embraced the foolishness of atheism and still held his head intellectually high. In doing so he could have concluded that there is neither right nor wrong, and that anything sexual — whether it is pornography, adultery, bestiality, fornication, or homosexuality is morally acceptable. For such a belief, somehow likening men to goats and tortoises is an appropriate analogy.

---

4. Ibid.

# CHAPTER TEN

# THE STRANGE MR. TWAIN

It's easy to become confused by Mark Twain's spiritual life. The word "twain" means two, and it seems appropriate for him because there seems to be two Twains. It seems that he believed in God and wrote congenial pieces such as the dairies of Adam and Eve. At one time in his life, he also spoke well of Jesus, saying that He was the only true Christian. He raised money to build a Presbyterian Church in Nevada in 1864, and said, "The goodness, the justice, and the mercy of God are manifested in His works."[1] But later in life for some reason he became venomous toward the Bible and God. There's perhaps a good reason for this change of heart.

In August of 2012, I had booked a camera crew to interview TLC's famous Duggar family (*19 Kids and Counting*) at their home

---

1. http://freethought.mbdojo.com/twain.html.

in Arkansas. A year or so earlier we met up with them in Washington DC, interviewed them about their faith in God, and filmed them learning how to open-air preach in front of the White House.

Three days before our flight to their home in Arkansas I was happy that I had everything in order. We had a permit to film at the local university. We had booked a room to screen our "180" movie to the students. A predicted hurricane looked like it wouldn't reach as far west as Arkansas, and so the weather was going to be fine and warm. Everything was perfect. That is, until I received an email from Jim Bob Duggar during the evening saying that he suspected that I had booked the filming permits at the wrong university. Sure enough, I had mistaken Arkansas State University for the University of Arkansas.

I consoled myself that Eddie, my director, could handle new permits. He had the know-how and had arranged the ones at Arkansas State. I would contact him in the morning. That night I dreamed that I didn't have an air ticket or boarding pass for the flight from California to Arkansas. I was running frantically around the inside of the airport carrying an oversized camera, was lost, and for some reason had a bleeding finger. Thankfully, I woke up and decided to check my email. There was one from Eddie saying that a rat had burst a water line in his house the previous day and had caused major damage. He had a hole in his ceiling and ripped up carpet. He said that he wished he was joking, but he had to take the day off.

Just before I received the email from Eddie, I was waiting by our back gate for my daughter and grandchildren to arrive. I had our dog on a leash, which I held with my left hand with a cup of hot tea in my right hand. Suddenly, the youngest appeared at the gate, looked at me and said, "High five!" I was taken back that a little girl would say such a thing. I quickly swapped the cup of tea to my left hand to accommodate her. Her sudden appearance made the dog excited, which caused the leash to jerk, spilling hot tea over the animal and down my shirt. It was then my granddaughter repeated her greeting. She had said, "I'm five!"

I couldn't help but think of Frank Sinatra's "That's life. That's what all the people say — riding high in April, shot down in May."

That's so true about life. One moment we are rejoicing because everything is going so well, then in a moment of time we are covered in hot tea. This happens regularly in daily life for most of us, with broken-down cars, appliances that won't work, sickness in the family, power cuts, bad weather, and unexpected bills. Some are serious, others just a little storm in a hot teacup. That's life.

But now and then we are blindsided by devastation with perhaps the death of a precious loved one. Tragically, a young Mark Twain had more than his share of these life-shattering storms:

> He was the sixth of seven children but only three of his sibling's survived childhood: his brother Orion (1825–1897), Henry, who died in a riverboat explosion (1838–1858), and Pamela (1827–1904). His sister Margaret (1833–1839) died when he was three, and his brother Benjamin (1832–1842) died three years later. Another brother, Pleasant (1828–1829), died at six months. In 1847, when Twain was 11, his father died of pneumonia.[2]

Twain's spirituality was typical of millions who go to church, believe in God, pray, give money to good causes, show kindness to others, all the while believing that they are doing the Christian thing. God to them is a Helpful Friend. They go to Him when something is needed or when something goes wrong. He isn't the God of the Bible — the One who is wrath-filled at our sins, warning us to repent because of the reality of hell. He is more loving, kind, and merciful. He is nice and He makes no moral demands.

An intellectual faith in this god is held by millions and can sustain the professed believer until the big storms come. Mr. Twain lived a fine life with light to moderate winds, until the tempests gathered later in his life:

> In 1894, the publishing company that Twain had founded with his nephew Charles L. Webster finally went belly-up after ten difficult years of constant financial strain.

---

2. http://umanitoba.academia.edu/EdKleiman/Papers/1243741/Two_Fictions_Mark_Twain_and_Samuel_Clemens_1993_.

Twain was nearly bankrupt. "The calamity that comes is never the one we had prepared ourselves for," he wrote to his wife. A close friend, the businessman Henry Huttleston Rogers, stepped in and took over his finances. Under the plan that Rogers created, Twain was not legally obligated to pay back his creditors. He courageously decided to do so anyway, and took up a two-year lecture tour to pay off his debts.

Olivia Langdon Clemens
(Photo courtesy of Library of Congress)

In 1896, while the author was still away on tour, Twain's 24-year-old daughter Susy Clemens died of meningitis. Twain had been especially close to Susy, an outspoken girl who often critiqued his lectures and work. He was utterly devastated by her death, which marked the end of his most successful period as a writer. Though he continued to lecture, write, and travel for most of his life, he never again had the kind of success he enjoyed with his travelogues and Huckleberry Finn. Then in 1904, things got even worse when Twain's beloved wife Livy died after a two-year illness. "I cannot reproduce Livy's face in my mind's eye," he wrote in his diary on 1 July 1904, just a few weeks after her death. "I was never in my life able to reproduce a face. It is a curious infirmity — & now at last I realize it is a calamity."[1]

In some later writings in the 1890s, he was less optimistic about the goodness of God, observing that "if our Maker is all-powerful for good or evil, He is not in His right mind."

Then the dark storm clouds thickened and lightning struck:

---

3. Albert Bigelow Paine, *Mark Twain: A Biography*, http://ebooks.adelaide.edu.au/t/twain/mark/paine/chapter232.html.

Olivia's death in 1904 and Jean's on December 24, 1909, deepened his gloom. On May 20, 1909, his close friend Henry Rogers died suddenly.[4]

The passing of his believed wife was a deathblow. The tragic details were given in *The New York Times*, June 7, 1904:

MARK TWAIN'S WIFE DEAD

Mrs. Clemens Expires Suddenly in Italy — Married to the Author in 1870.

FLORENCE, June 6. — Mrs. Samuel M. [sic] Clemens, the wife of Mark Twain, the American author and lecturer, died from syncope here last evening. Half an hour before her death she had conversed cheerfully with her husband. Mrs. Clemens died painlessly. The body has been embalmed, and will be sent to the United States. Mr. Clemens kneels continually by the coffin. He speaks to no one.

It was on account of his wife's poor health that Mr. Clemens decided several months ago to live in Italy. Mr. and Mrs. Clemens arrived at Florence last Nov. 8. A month later is was announced that Mrs. Clemens had been so indisposed since her arrival in Italy that no one outside her family had been allowed to see her. In the latter part of January it was said that her condition had greatly improved.

Mrs. Clemens was Miss Olivia L. Langdon. She was a native of Elmira, N. Y., and was married to Mr. Clemens in 1870.

About a year later, he wrote of her death in an article titled "The Death of my Wife":

It is one of the mysteries of our nature that a man, all unprepared, can receive a thunder-stroke like that and live. There is but one reasonable explanation of it. The intellect is stunned by the shock, and but gropingly gathers the meaning of the words. The power to realize their full import

---

4. J.R. LeMaster, James D. Wilson, Christie Graves Hamric, *The Mark Twain Encyclopedia* (New York: Taylor & Francis, 1993), p. 28.

is mercifully wanting. The mind has a dumb sense of vast loss — that is all. It will take mind and memory months, and possibly years, to gather together the details, and thus learn and know the whole extent of the loss. A man's house burns down. The smoking wreckage represents only a ruined home that was dear through years of use and pleasant associations. By and by, as the days and weeks go on, first he misses this, then that, then the other thing. And, when he casts about for it, he finds that it was in that house. Always it is an essential — there was but one of its kind. It cannot be replaced. It was in that house. It is irrevocably lost. He did not realize that it was an essential when he had it; he only discovers it now when he finds himself balked, hampered, by its absence. It will be years before the tale of lost essentials is complete, and not till then can he truly know the magnitude of his disaster.[5]

It was at this point is his life that he clearly became openly angry at God and poured his bitterness onto paper. He believed in God, no doubt in his mind he had lived a good moral life, and he had given to the church. He had lost the ability to enjoy the marital bed, lost all of his wealth, was feeling the pains of an aging body, and now death had taken his friends, his precious family, and now his beloved wife. His only refuge was bitterness toward the God who had allowed these calamities. He had good reason to be depressed. He has spent years nipping at the hand that fed him and the only hand that could rescue him from death. He had dug his own grave, and now he must lie in it, with the bitterness of bitterness:

In the autobiography itself, Twain mixes news and history, using something from the "infernal newspapers" as a jumping-off point for his dictation. For example, the American war in the Philippines was still going on in 1906, and Twain read that American troops cornered 600 of the Moro tribe, including women and children, in a volcanic crater.

5. http://www.everywritersresource.com/writingsense/2010/11/the-death-of-my-wife-by-mark-twain/.

Leonard Wood — Twain called him Theodore Roosevelt's "fragrant pet" — gave the order to "kill or capture" the 600.[6]

In March of 1906, when speaking of this massacre, Clemens takes the hymn "Onward Christians Soldiers" and applies it to the U.S. Army. Was Mr. Clemens so ignorant that he thought that the war in which Christians are involved was a physical war and that our mandate was to kill rather than love our enemies? He said,

> General Wood was present and looking on. His order had been. "Kill or capture those savages." Apparently our little army considered that the "or" left them authorized to kill or capture according to taste, and that their taste had remained what it had been for eight years, in our army out there — the taste of Christian butchers.[7]

How wrong it was of him to call those he considered to be vicious, bloodthirsty killers "Christians." Another reviewer of his writings, said,

> There is a perception that Twain spent his final years basking in the adoration of fans. The autobiography will perhaps show that it wasn't such a happy time. He spent six months of the last year of his life writing a manuscript full of vitriol, saying things that he'd never said about anyone in print before. It really is 400 pages of bile.[8]

He had loved and lost and became an embittered and angry man. It was C.S. Lewis who said,

> To love at all is to be vulnerable. Love anything and your heart will be wrung and possibly broken. If you want to make sure of keeping it intact you must give it to no one, not even an animal. Wrap it carefully round with hobbies

---

6. http://www.independent.co.uk/arts-entertainment/books/news/after-keeping-us-waiting-for-a-century-mark-twain-will-finally-reveal-all-1980695.html.

7. http://www.is.wayne.edu/mnissani/cr/moro.htm.

8. http://www.independent.co.uk/arts-entertainment/books/news/after-keeping-us-waiting-for-a-century-mark-twain-will-finally-reveal-all-1980695.html.

and little luxuries; avoid all entanglements. Lock it up safe in the casket or coffin of your selfishness. But in that casket, safe, dark, motionless, airless, it will change. It will not be broken; it will become unbreakable, impenetrable, irredeemable. To love is to be vulnerable.[9]

Twain certainly left himself vulnerable. He didn't believe the Bible, so he didn't have the comfort of the Scriptures. They weren't a lamp to his feet and a light to his path because he had blown out the only candle in the room. He was lost in the darkness of this life with no map for any sense of direction. Neither did he have faith in God. He didn't trust in the Lord with all of his heart. Instead he had leaned to his own understanding. Those who refuse the security of trust in God will eventually find themselves insecure and alone, left to their doubts and fears. And the biggest fear as a man approaches death is the nagging dread that hell may be real, that God may be holy, and the Savior he rejected was his only hope of salvation.

Jesus warned of life's inevitable storms and what would happen to those who ignored His teachings. He said:

> "Therefore whoever hears these sayings of Mine, and does them, I will liken him to a wise man who built his house on the rock: and the rain descended, the floods came, and the winds blew and beat on that house; and it did not fall, for it was founded on the rock.
>
> "But everyone who hears these sayings of Mine, and does not do them, will be like a foolish man who built his house on the sand: and the rain descended, the floods came, and the winds blew and beat on that house; and it fell. And great was its fall" (Matthew 7:24–27).

---

9. C.S. Lewis, *The Four Loves,* http://www.goodreads.com/quotes/3058-to-love-at-all-is-to-be-vulnerable-love-anything.

# CHAPTER ELEVEN

# DID MARK TWAIN BECOME AN ATHEIST?

The "new" atheists (the self-styled "freethinkers") aren't new at all. They are old. Thomas Paine was considered by most atheists to be one of the first if not the first "freethinker," a great intellectual mind who challenged God and the Bible. Twain was a pale clone of Paine, and Paine wasn't an atheist.

Popular ex-atheist, Christopher Hitchens (who tragically went to meet his Maker in 2011), said of Thomas Paine,

> . . . when both rights and reason are under several kinds of open and covert attack, the life and writing of Thomas Paine will always be part of the arsenal on which we shall need to depend.[1]

---

1. Quoted in John Barrell, "The Positions He Takes," *London Review of Books*, 28.23 (November 30, 2006). Retrieved on July 20, 2007.

Thomas Paine reviled Christianity. He said, "It is from the Bible that man has learned cruelty, rapine[2] and murder; for the belief of a cruel God makes a cruel man."[3] He blamed the Scriptures for corruption and cruelty: "The Bible: a history of wickedness that has served to corrupt and brutalize mankind."[4] He was offended by the New Testament's virgin birth, saying, "What is it the New Testament teaches us? To believe that the Almighty committed debauchery with a woman engaged to be married; and the belief of this debauchery is called faith."[5] He also said,

> As to the Christian system of faith, it appears to me as a species of atheism — a sort of religious denial of God. It professed to believe in man rather than in God. It is as near to atheism as twilight to darkness. It introduces between man and his Maker an opaque body, which it calls a Redeemer, as the moon introduces her opaque self between the earth and the sun, and it produces by this means a religious or irreligious eclipse of the light. It has put the whole orbit of reason into shade.[6]

It is because of his anti-Christian philosophy that many contemporary atheists latch onto Paine as a founding father of modern atheism, yet (as with so many heroes of modern atheism) Paine wasn't foolish enough to be an atheist. He believed in the existence of God:

> The moral duty of man consists in imitating the moral goodness and beneficence of God manifested in the creation toward all his creatures. That seeing, as we daily do, the goodness of God to all men, it is an example calling upon all men to practice the same toward each other.[7]

---

2. The use of force to seize somebody else's property.
3. Thomas Paine, as quoted by Joseph Lewis in *Inspiration and Wisdom from the Writings of Thomas Paine* (New York: Freethought Press Association, 1954).
4. Thomas Paine, *The Age of Reason* (1793–5), quoted from Jonathon Green, *The Cassell Dictionary of Cynical Quotations* (London: Cassell; New York, NY: Sterling Pub., 1994).
5. Paine, *The Age of Reason* (1794).
6. Ibid.
7. Ibid.

Were man impressed as fully and as strongly as he ought to be with the belief of a God, his moral life would be regulated by the force of that belief; he would stand in awe of God and of himself, and would not do the thing that could not be concealed from either. . . . This is Deism.[8]

Reposing confidence in my Creator, God.[9]

I die in perfect composure and resignation to the will of my Creator, God.[10]

I trouble not myself about the manner of future existence. I content myself with believing, even to positive conviction, that the power that gave me existence is able to continue it in any form and manner he pleases, either with or without this body.[11]

I consider myself in the hands of my Creator, and that he will dispose of me after this life consistently with his justice and goodness.[12]

Pain is famous in atheist circles because of his book *Age of Reason.* This is from the opening chapter:

I believe in one God, and no more; and I hope for happiness beyond this life.

I believe in the equality of man; and I believe that religious duties consist in doing justice, loving mercy, and endeavoring to make our fellow-creatures happy.

But, lest it should be supposed that I believe in many other things in addition to these, I shall, in the progress of this work, declare the things I do not believe, and my reasons for not believing them. I do not believe in the creed

---

8. Ibid.
9. From the will of Thomas Paine, https://familycouncil.org/?p=6440.
10. Ibid.
11. Paine, *The Age of Reason.*
12. From Paine's essay, "My Private Thoughts on a Future State," http://www.deism.com/paine_essay_future_state.htm.

**Birthplace of Mark Twain, Florida, Missouri**
(Photo courtesy of Library of Congress)

professed by the Jewish church, by the Roman church, by the Greek church, by the Turkish church, by the Protestant church, nor by any church that I know of. My own mind is my own church.[13]

The atheistic website "Infidels.org" concedes of Paine:

> The *Age of Reason,* instead of being an Atheistic work, as popularly supposed, was written to oppose Atheism. In a letter to Samuel Adams, Paine says: "The people of France were running headlong into Atheism, and I had the work translated into their own language, to stop them in that career, and fix them in the first article of every man's creed, who has any creed at all — I believe in God."[14]

Ron Powers, in his book *Mark Twain: A Life*, said,

> One writer in particular influenced Mark Twain's intellectual development. Thomas Paine, the British born

13. http://www.ushistory.org/paine/reason/reason1.htm, *Age of Reason,* by Thomas Paine, part first, section 1.

14. http://www.infidels.org/library/historical/john_remsburg/six_historic_americans/chapter_1.html#1.

The boyhood home of Mark Twain was this gray house in Missouri, described as Tom Sawyer's home in Mark Twain's best-known story, "The Adventures of Tom Sawyer." (Photo courtesy of Library of Congress)

American patriot. . . . In *The Age of Reason,* Paine's icy 1795 deconstruction of the "heathen mythology" that was the Christian faith, Sam was mesmerized by a rebuttal to the terrifying sermons of his Presbyterian boyhood. He "read it with fear and hesitation but marveling at its fearlessness and wonderful power."[15]

There was no doubt that Twain was greatly influenced by the writing of Thomas Paine:

> *The Bible According to Mark Twain* (1995) brought together Twain's most important religious writings, the most important anthology to date of Twain's religious musings including texts not previously published. The volume, as the editors note, demonstrates how Twain's conflict between religion and science was as a typical thinker in the nineteenth century, influenced by Paine and Darwin.[16]

Another writer put Paine's influence on Twain this way,

> It is nearly impossible to exaggerate the impact of *The Age of Reason* on the mind of Mark Twain. He read it when he was twenty-one or twenty-two, and apparently not again until he was in his seventies, yet its pristine

---

15. Ron Powers, *Mark Twain: A Life* (New York: Free Press, 2005), p. 81.
16. http://www.twainweb.net/filelist/skeptic.html.

meanings — and even phraseology — were wedged into his memory.[17]

So, did Twain become an atheist? Did he go one further than Paine and deny the existence of God? There is no doubt in the mind of most atheists that the brilliant satirist was one of their own, and they have piles of godless quotes from his own mouth and pen to back up their claim. However, some haven't such confidence, and for some reason question his atheism.

When asked "Are you of the opinion that Mark Twain was an atheist?" Cliff Walker, the editor of *Positive Atheism Magazine*, answered,

> No. . . . Part of the time he sure seemed like an atheist (such as the poem "Contract with Mrs. T.K. Beecher") but other times he seemed like a theist or at least one who embraced the supernatural.

Others say,

> Mark Twain had strong opinions on religion. He was not one to be swayed by religious propaganda or sermons. However, Mark Twain was not considered an atheist. He was evidently against conventional religion; and the traditions and dogma that prevail within religion.[18]

Mr. Twain once said, "Blasphemy? No, it is not blasphemy. If God is as vast as that, he is above blasphemy; if He is as little as that, He is beneath it."[19] So much of his philosophy has found its way into the worldview of today's atheists. From Dawkins to the teenage atheist who has just arrived at his atheist beliefs, they echo Twain's thoughts about God being a thug and that He is above blasphemy — almost word-for-word, not knowing that the man from whom they came wasn't an atheist.

---

17. http://www.compedit.com/theory_of_realism.htm.

18. http://quotations.about.com/od/marktwainquotes/a/twainreligion.htm.

19. Albert Bigelow Paine, *Mark Twain: A Biography*, http://ebooks.adelaide.edu.au/t/twain/mark/paine/chapter232.

Despite the mass of venomous quotes about God, the Bible, heaven, and hell, confusion sets in when one considers his following words:

> No man that has ever lived has done a thing to please God — primarily. It was done to please himself, then God next.[20]

> Man proposes, but God blocks the game.[21]

> God pours out love upon all with a lavish hand — but He reserves vengeance for His very own.[22]

> None of us can be as great as God, but any of us can be as good.[23]

> It is by the goodness of God that in our country we have those three unspeakably precious things: freedom of speech, freedom of conscience, and the prudence never to practice either of them.[24]

In reacting to my contention that Twain wasn't an atheist, an atheist responded:

> You can't really be this stupid. Every quote you supplied from Twain does not support the idea that he believed in God, but rather they all advance the ideas that a belief in God is absurd. All the quotes sound like they came from a thoughtful atheist.[25]

Another atheist said, "Your 'sarcasm detector' is severely malfunctioning. Twain was saying that 'God's' behavior is no better than

---

20. Paine, *Mark Twain, a Biography*, http://www.marktwainhannibal.com/twain/quotes/.
21. Letter to Jean Clemens, June 19, 1908, http://www.twainquotes.com/God.html.
22. Mark Twain's Notebook, http://www.twainquotes.com/God.html.
23. Mark Twain's Notebook, 1902–1903, http://www.twainquotes.com/God.html
24. The Official Website of Mark Twain, http://www.cmgww.com/historic/twain/about/quotes3.htm
25. https://www.blogger.com/comment.g?blogID=5823596693953871104&postID=7667681603641400176.

any human's behavior . . . malevolent, petty, jealous, etc. You make me laugh." Another said, "I understand sarcasm is much harder to detect in writing, but Mark Twain seems to make it quite clear, Mr. Comfort. He's insulting God in each one of those quotes, and calls into question how people can worship such a being."[26]

Do they have a point? Was Mark Twain an atheist who used the sharp tongue of sarcasm to express his atheism? The following quotes tend to cloud the issue even further. He said,

> I believe in God the Almighty. . . . I think the good-ness, the justice, and the mercy of God are manifested in His works.[27]

> When I think of the suffering which I see around me, and how it wrings my heart; and then remember what a drop in the ocean this is, compared with the measureless Atlantics of misery which God has to see every day, my resentment is roused against those thoughtless people who are so glib to glorify God, yet never to have a word of pity for Him.[28]

> Every man is wholly honest to himself and to God, but not to anyone else.[29]

However, the flowing words banish the clouds of confusion and give light on the subject. In 1906 he wrote:

> Let us now consider the real God, the genuine God, the sublime and supreme God, the authentic Creator of the real universe, whose remotenesses are visited by comets only — comets unto which incredible distant Neptune is merely an outpost, a Sandy Hook to homeward-bound specters of the deeps of space that have not glimpsed it before for genera-tions — a universe not made with hands and suited to an

---

26. Ibid.
27. http://philosophiesofmen.blogspot.com/2012/01/mark-twain-and-god-almighty.html.
28. William E. Phipps, *Mark Twain's Religion* (Indianapolis, IN: Bobbs-Merrill, 1973), p. 276.
29. http://www.twainquotes.com/Honesty.html.

astronomical nursery, but spread abroad through illimitable reaches of space by the fiat of the real God just mentioned by comparison with whom the gods of those myriads infest the feeble imaginations of men are as a swarm of gnats scattered and lost in the infinitudes of the empty sky.[30]

Mark Twain's contention wasn't with the Creator of the universe. He was no fool. He knew that it is scientifically impossible for nothing to create everything. His problem was with the *identity* of that Maker. His concept of God was far grander than the God of the Bible, whom he found to be morally offensive. Twain's idea of God wasn't one that was omnipresent, hearing every word, seeing every deed, and holding man morally accountable. His concept of the Creator was one who didn't bother Himself with such trivialities as right and wrong, justice and truth.

**The Only True God**

Thank God He doesn't leave the humble in confusion. He hears their cry. It was Charles Spurgeon who rightly said, "To believe Him that cannot lie, and trust in Him that cannot fail, is a kind of wisdom that none but fools will laugh at."[31] What a pity Twain embraced Payne above the Bible. What a tragedy that he was a stranger to the new birth. Such thoughts about him turn my thoughts to you. Forgive me for hounding you, but do you know the Lord? Have you been born again? Jesus answered,

> "Most assuredly, I say to you, unless one is born of water and the Spirit, he cannot enter the kingdom of God. That which is born of the flesh is flesh, and that which is born of the Spirit is spirit. Do not marvel that I said to you, 'You must be born again' " (John 3:5–7).

The Christian Church is built on the person of Jesus and on His teachings, and He said that each of us must be born again to enter

---

30. Paine, *Mark Twain, A Biography.*
31. C.H. Spurgeon, "Elijah's Please No. 1832," https://bible.org/book/export/html/2625.

heaven. If we don't experience the new birth we will end up in a terrible place called "hell," so it's vital that we understand what it means to be born again.

Perhaps the best way to explain it is to say what it's not.

It's not infant baptism. It's not adult baptism. It's not being a member of the Presbyterian, Methodist, Catholic, Anglican, or any other church. It's not being a member of the Salvation Army or any religion or denomination or cult. It doesn't mean to believe in God as the Creator or in Jesus as an historical figure.

The first time we were born, it was radical. We didn't exist, and then life was sparked and suddenly we existed. The new birth is just as radical.

We need to be born again if we are black or white, rich or poor, tall or short, Jew or Gentile, Moslem or Hindu, or an adulterer, a homosexual, a transvestite, a fornicator, a thief, or a liar. It makes no difference if you are a president, a pope, a priest, a pastor, a paparazzi, or a prayerful Protestant — you must be born again . . . or you will not enter heaven — you have Jesus' promise on that.

If your heart is beating, you must be born of the Spirit . . . according to Jesus. If this makes you angry, your issue is with Him and not with me. I'm simply telling you what He said. Am I your enemy because I tell you the truth? Atheist Penn Jillette said, "How much do you have to hate somebody to not proselytize? How much do you have to hate someone to believe that everlasting life is possible and not tell them that?"[32]

When someone is born of the Spirit they don't just "believe" in God, they come to *know* Him. Do you know God or do you just know "about" Him? Have you obeyed the gospel and been born again? Don't fool yourself because you can't afford to be wrong about this. It's your eternal salvation that's at stake here.

The Bible says the time will come when "the Lord Jesus is revealed from heaven with His mighty angels, in flaming fire taking vengeance on those who do not know God, and on those who do

---

32. http://thegospelcoalition.org/blogs/justintaylor/2009/11/17/how-much-do-you-have-to-hate-somebody-to-not-proselytize/.

not obey the gospel of our Lord Jesus Christ. These shall be punished with everlasting destruction from the presence of the Lord and from the glory of His power, when He comes, in that Day, to be glorified in His saints and to be admired among all those who believe, because our testimony among you was believed" (2 Thessalonians 1:7–10).

## Young or Old?

You are flying across beautiful New Zealand with about a dozen American tourists in a small chartered plane. As you gaze at a massive snow-capped and rugged mountain in the distance, the pilot quickly brings you back to reality. His voice is noticeably strained as he says that he is having serious problems controlling the plane. He soberly says that he is going to ditch the plane and that you must listen carefully if you want to live.

He calms your fears by telling you that the maker of the plane has made sure that there are enough parachutes under the seats for every passenger. He tells you to quickly reach under your seat and to put one on because the jump will happen at any moment.

Without warning, the plane suddenly drops a horrifying thousand feet, creating chaos by sending cups and boiling coffee flying, burning passengers, and seriously injuring a flight attendant. You don't need any more convincing that he is telling you the truth. You quickly reach under your seat. The parachute is attached exactly where the pilot said it would be.

The man next to you is wearing earphones and watching a movie on his laptop. You tap him on the arm and say, "Excuse me. You had better take the earphones off." Then you explain what the pilot has just said. To your amazement the man says, "I don't believe him. He's lying. I believe that this plane had no maker." You are dumbfounded and ask why he would believe such a crazy thing. He answers that he thinks it fell together by chance. Then he said that the instruction booklet was bogus because he had found mistakes in it. When you ask him to be specific he smugly points to the word "neighbour," and the word "colour." You tell him that in New Zealand and the rest of the English-speaking world, both those words are spelled that way.

Only America drops the "u." He laughs at you and calls you an idiot for believing that, adding that he thought the graphics showing how to put the parachute on were simplistic.

You become very concerned that he is going to die if he stays with the plane, so you warn him that he will die without the parachute. He says that you are using fear tactics; you have a death wish, that you are a weak-minded and manipulative person who is fearful of dying.

Then he asks you if you think the plane is old or young. You tell him that the issue is unimportant to you. You just want him to put the parachute on, and then he can talk about the age of the plane.

He insists that it's extremely old, and that proves that no one made it. You reason with him by telling him that the chaos on the flight backs up what the pilot has told the passengers and so does the reality of the parachute under the seat. He thinks the chaos on the flight is the way it should be. Then he laughs at you and goes back to his movie.

Here is a proud and arrogant man who will find in time that what you have said is true. You look across the aisle and see another passenger who is enjoying a movie, and he's not wearing a parachute. You reach out and tap him on the arm. . . .

# CHAPTER TWELVE

# TWAIN AND THE TEN COMMANDMENTS

Here are Mark Twain's promised thoughts regarding The Ten Commandments:

The Ten Commandments were made for man alone. We should think it strange if they had been made for *all* the animals.

We should say "Thou shalt not kill" is too general, too sweeping. It includes the field mouse and the butterfly. They *can't* kill. And it includes the tiger, which can't *help* it.

It is a case of Temperament and Circumstance again. You can arrange no circumstances that can move the field mouse and the butterfly to kill; their temperaments will ill keep them unaffected by temptations to kill, they can avoid that crime without an effort. But it isn't so with the tiger. Throw a lamb in his way when he is hungry, and his temperament will compel him to kill it.

Butterflies and field mice are common among men; they can't kill, their temperaments make it impossible. There are tigers among men, also. Their temperaments move them to violence, and when Circumstance furnishes the opportunity and the powerful motive, they kill. They can't help it.

No penal law can deal out *justice*; it must deal out injustice in every instance. Penal laws have a high value, in that they protect — in a considerable measure — the multitude of the gentle-natured from the violent minority.

For a penal law is a Circumstance. It is a warning which intrudes and stays a would-be murderer's hand — sometimes. Not always, but in many and many a case. It can't stop the *real* man-tiger; nothing can do that. Slade had 26 deliberate murders on his soul when he finally went to his death on the scaffold.[1] He would kill a man for a trifle; or for nothing. He loved to kill. It was his temperament. He did not make his temperament, God gave it him at his birth. Gave it him and said Thou shalt not kill. It was like saying Thou shalt not eat. Both appetites were given him at birth. He could be obedient and starve both up to a certain point, but that was as far as he could go. Another man could go further; but not Slade.

Holmes, the Chicago monster,[2] inveigled some dozens of men and women into his obscure quarters and

---

1. Joseph Alfred "Jack" Slade: "Slade's exploits spawned numerous legends, many of them false. His image (especially via Mark Twain in *Roughing It*) as the vicious killer of up to 26 victims was greatly exaggerated: Only one killing by Slade (that of Andrew Ferrin, above ) is undisputed." Rottenberg, *Death of a Gunfighter*, p. 270–275. http://en.wikipedia.org/wiki/Joseph_Alfred_Slade#cite_note-12.

2. "Herman Webster Mudgett (May 16, 1861–May 7, 1896), better known under the name of Dr. Henry Howard Holmes, was one of the first documented American serial killers in the modern sense of the term. In Chicago at the time of the 1893 World's Fair, Holmes opened a hotel which he had designed and built for himself specifically with murder in mind, and which was the location of many of his murders. While he confessed to 27 murders, of which nine were confirmed, his actual body count could be as high as 200." http://en.wikipedia.org/wiki/H._H._Holmes#cite_note-dope-3.

privately butchered them. Holmes's inborn nature was such that whenever he had what seemed a reasonably safe opportunity to kill a stranger he couldn't successfully resist the temptation to do it.

Justice was finally meted out to Slade and to Holmes. That is what the newspapers said. It is a common phrase, and a very old one. But it probably isn't true. When a man is hanged for slaying *one* man that phrase comes into service and we learn that justice was meted out to the slayer. But Holmes slew sixty. There seems to be a discrepancy in this distribution of justice. If Holmes got justice, the other man got 59 times more than justice.

But the phrase is wrong, anyway. The *word* is the wrong word. Criminal courts do not dispense "justice" — they *can't*; they only dispense protections to the community. It is all they can do. (1905 or 1906) [3]

After saying that the Ten Commandments were made for man alone, Mark Twain says, "We should think it strange if they had been made for *all* the animals." The use of the word all (in italics) seems to reveal that either Twain was a believer in evolution or that he was influenced by its erroneous belief that man is an animal. He is not. Animals have animal instincts. Man is unique in that he was made in the image of God with a sense of moral responsibility. We set up court systems with judges and laws to give justice to those who transgress those laws. Animals don't do that because they aren't made in the image of God.

God gave a physical Law, written in stone tablets and handed down to Moses. But he also gave a law, written on the fleshly tablets of the human heart. Every human being has a God-given sense of right and wrong. We inherently know that it is morally wrong to commit adultery, to lie, steal, and to murder. This is why we would think that it would be strange if God had given the Ten Commandments to the animals. They were uniquely given to man, because man is unique in that he only is made in the image of God.

---

3. John Sutton Tuckey, editor, *Mark Twain's Fables of Man* (Berkeley, CA: University of California Press, 1972).

We need to be continually reminded that Mark Twain didn't believe that the Bible was the Word of God. He didn't believe that the Ten Commandments were written by the finger of God onto two stone tablets and given to Moses. So when the Bible tells us that man was made in the image of God, that holds no credibility in his mind. Yet he writes as though it does, and he does so for his own ends. He quotes, "Thou shalt not kill," but doesn't see the need to stay with the integrity of Scripture and explain that the word "kill" in this context clearly means to "murder." Lions don't *murder* lambs. They kill them. A cat doesn't *murder* a mouse. The cat kills the mouse, but he's not culpable. To say that he is morally responsible is to charge the cat with a crime, and therefore justice should ensue. Look at how Scripture makes this moral division and explains why it exists:

> Whoever sheds man's blood, by man his blood shall be
> shed; for in the image of God He made man (Genesis 9:6).

The word "murder" is reserved for man, because he alone is made in the likeness of God. Animals are not moral creatures because they aren't made in the image of God. So he is trying to build a case against God and His Law on a false premise. He says that the butterfly and the mouse can't kill, but the tiger can, concluding that both are cases of what he calls "Temperament and Circumstance." He says that we can't arrange any circumstance in which both would be tempted to kill, saying, "They can avoid that crime without an effort. But it isn't so with the tiger. Throw a lamb in his way when he is hungry, and his temperament will compel him to kill it." What is this "crime" of which he is speaking? Again, there is no crime when a tiger kills. This is because no law has been violated by the animal — because it is an animal. It's not made in the image of God with a sense of justice, truth, and righteousness. Only man is morally accountable because "the work of the law is written on his heart" and his conscience is in agreement with that Law:

> For when Gentiles, who do not have the law, by nature
> do the things in the law, these, although not having the law,

are a law to themselves, who show the work of the law written in their hearts, their conscience also bearing witness, and between themselves their thoughts accusing or else excusing them) in the day when God will judge the secrets of men by Jesus Christ, according to my gospel (Romans 2:14–16).

It is upon *mens rea* that our penal system is built. *Mens rea* is Latin for "guilty mind." In criminal law, it is viewed as one of the necessary elements of a crime. The standard, common law test of criminal liability is usually expressed in the Latin phrase *actus non facit reum nisi mens sit rea*, which means "the act does not make a person guilty unless the mind is also guilty." In other words, human beings who murder do so knowing that it is morally wrong and they are therefore culpable despite their "God-given" temperament.

Mark Twain then continues to build his case on a wrong foundation. He says, "Penal laws have a high value, in that they protect — in a considerable measure — the multitude of the gentle-natured from the violent minority. For a penal law is a Circumstance. It is a warning which intrudes and stays a would-be murderer's hand — sometimes."[4]

Penal law's high purpose isn't to protect. It is to punish. If a man sheds blood, his blood is to be shed. If man is an animal and not morally responsible, then he isn't culpable. He can't help committing murder. He is like the poor tiger that "can't help it," and he is therefore not responsible, and should not be punished. He is rather to be rehabilitated, and if he is placed in prison this should be enough warning to would-be murderers.

No, penal law's high purpose isn't to protect society from evil men. It is to see that justice is done, and that means retribution not rehabilitation. Again, if he sheds blood, his blood should be shed. If that retribution is seen as a warning to would-be murderers, that is merely good fruit, but it isn't the life-giving root.

Twain then combines his two errors. He wrongly believes that the law's purpose is to warn would-be murderers, and he believes

---

4. Mark Twain, *Fables of Man*, "The Ten Commandments," www.atheist-community. org/library/articles/read.php?id=731.

that men and tigers have the same moral values. In speaking of the law and a mass murderer, he says,

> It can't stop the *real* man-tiger; nothing can do that. Slade had 26 deliberate murders on his soul when he finally went to his death on the scaffold.[5]

So Slade wasn't a murderer, made in the image of God. He was a man-tiger; a poor unfortunate animal who couldn't help but commit murder. Twain says of this wicked man, "He loved to kill. It was his temperament. He did not make his temperament; God gave it him at his birth. Gave it him and said Thou shalt not kill. It was like saying Thou shalt not eat. Both appetites were given him at birth."[6]

So who is the real criminal? It is the God of the Bible. The One who gave the Law that said "Thou shalt not kill." The One Twain doesn't believe exists.

Then Mr. Twain sides with another mass murderer against God by further removing any sense of culpability:

> Holmes's inborn nature was such that whenever he had what seemed a reasonably safe opportunity to kill a stranger he couldn't successfully resist the temptation to do it.[7]

He then complains that justice wasn't done when Holmes was executed, because he gave one life when he had taken 59, complaining "There seems to be a discrepancy in this distribution of justice. If Holmes got justice, the other man got 59 times more than justice. But the phrase is wrong, anyway. The *word* is the wrong word. Criminal courts do not dispense 'justice' — they *can't*; they only dispense protections to the community. It is all they can do."[8]

He needn't worry. On Judgment Day, perfect justice will come for Holmes, for Slade, for Twain, and for each of us if we are not safe in Christ.

---

5. Ibid.
6. Ibid.
7. Ibid.
8. Ibid.

# CHAPTER THIRTEEN

# THE ILLEGITIMATE FOUNDING FATHER

Theist Mark Twain has been adopted as the illegitimate founding father of modern atheism. His blasphemous thoughts about God as being a "thug" and his venomous quotes about Jesus and religion are heralded as trumpet calls to convert to atheism. So let's look briefly at modern atheism for a few minutes.

I was on a live broadcast and a couple of people sat in on the program — an Irishman named Larry and his teenage son. Larry had been a fisherman in his youth and had lost an arm in machinery on his boat. At the end of the broadcast, I held up a sign that told the studio audience to applaud. Larry's son didn't applaud much. He was too busy looking at his one-armed dad as he tried to clap. The program had no sense of closure that day.

The sound of a one-armed man clapping produces as much sound as atheists produce when asked for scientific evidence to back up their claims of a world being brought into existence without a Creator. Of course, they think the same of those who believe that God exists. That's why they consider themselves to be atheists. But many are confused when it comes to the issue of faith. They don't understand that there can be a rational faith, based on solid evidence. We conclude that there is a Creator because creation could not have created itself. We know that there is an intelligent designer because nature is intelligently designed. To see such complexity in nature and come to the conclusion that there is no Creator is more than irrational, it is ridiculous.

So the existence of God isn't an issue. It doesn't need "faith." It merely needs eyes that can see "the invisible things of him from the creation of the world" (Romans 1:20; KJV). However, the legitimate question does arise as to why a Christian believes in heaven and hell and that he or she has everlasting life. Is it simply because the Bible says so and we blindly believe it?

Let's say I've been waiting for weeks to move into a newly built house. Time after time there were problems with the electrical work, to a point where I almost lost hope it would ever be done.

Finally I see a sight I can hardly believe. It is a signed note pinned to the door of the house, saying, "The electrical is done. You now have power. Flick the switch." I flick the switch and the power comes on! So I then conclude that the note was certainly authentic. That conclusion didn't come because I welled up some sort of belief in the note, but because the note proved itself to be true when the power came on.

God's note is the Bible. It says, "You will receive power when the Holy Spirit comes upon you. . . . I will give you a new heart. . . . Old things pass away, all things become new."

I believe the Bible, not because I welled up some sort of faith in its words, but because it said that God would make me a completely new person if I would repent and place my trust in Jesus alone. It authenticated itself as the Word of God by supernaturally doing what it said it would do. The power came on and transformed me instantly into a brand new person.

This didn't come about because of anything I did. It was a completely independent source of power that took me out of darkness and brought me into light. Therefore I can trust that every other promise in Scripture about heaven, hell, and everlasting life is utterly true altogether.

## Sell It All and Buy a Place in Heaven

The Bible is also evidence of God's existence. Anyone who approaches the Scriptures in search of truth will find it because those truths are axiomatic. The key to understanding the Bible is "context." For example, it would be easy to conclude from the Bible that we can earn our way to heaven. Jesus told the rich young ruler that he could have everlasting life by selling all of his goods and giving it to the poor:

> Now a certain ruler asked Him, saying, "Good Teacher, what shall I do to inherit eternal life?"
>
> So Jesus said to him, "Why do you call Me good? No one is good but One, that is, God. You know the commandments: 'Do not commit adultery,' 'Do not murder,' 'Do not steal,' 'Do not bear false witness,' 'Honor your father and your mother.' "
>
> And he said, "All these things I have kept from my youth."
>
> So when Jesus heard these things, He said to him, "You still lack one thing. Sell all that you have and distribute to the poor, and you will have treasure in heaven; and come, follow Me" (Luke 18:18–22).

At face value, this seems to be saying that we should sell what we have, give to the poor, and in exchange, God will give us everlasting life. However, in context we know that no one can be made right with God by any good works — that salvation is a free gift of God (see Ephesians 2:8–9). Rather, Jesus is using the Law to bring the knowledge of sin. He is holding up the mirror of the moral Law for the man to see his sin of covetousness.

It's essential that we approach Scripture *in context* with what the entire Bible says on any subject and allow the text to speak rather than shape it to what we believe it says. This is something the Bible calls correct "exegesis."

Here's some bad exegesis: Did you know that in Scripture written about 800 B.C., in a mere six verses the Bible mentions the following words: tires, chains, mufflers, hoods, bonnets, and rings:

> In that day the Lord will take away the bravery of their tinkling ornaments about their feet, and their cauls, and their round tires like the moon,
> The chains, and the bracelets, and the mufflers,
> The bonnets, and the ornaments of the legs, and the headbands, and the tablets, and the earrings,
> The rings, and nose jewels,
> The changeable suits of apparel, and the mantles, and the wimples, and the crisping pins,
> The glasses, and the fine linen, and the hoods, and the vails (Isaiah 3:18–23; KJV).

Anyone who has put chains on their tires in freezing conditions, repaired mufflers, or lifted the hood ("bonnet" down under) to replace piston rings could perhaps be convinced that the Scriptures are foreseeing the advent of the motor vehicle . . . if the verses are taken out of context.

In our zeal to convince the world that the Bible is the Word of God, we can use the Bible to say things that it doesn't say. Skeptics and atheists do the same thing in their zeal to present their case against God. Ex-atheist Christopher Hitchens, just before his tragic death of cancer, said,

> Atheism by itself is of course not a moral decision or a political one of any kind. It simply is the refusal to believe in a Supernatural dimension. For you to say of Nazism, that it was the implementation of the work of Charles Darwin is a filthy slander, undeserving of you and an insult to this audience. Darwin's thought was not taught in Germany. Darwinism wasn't derided in Germany along with

every other form of unbelief. All the great modern atheist thinkers: Darwin, Einstein and Freud were alike despised by the National Socialist Regime.[1]

Hitchens was either misrepresenting the truth or he was ignorant, and I have a hard time believing that such an educated and eloquent man could have been ignorant.

To understand the atheist we have to appreciate his worldview. He is of the persuasion that there is no God, and that there is no retribution for dishonesty. Dishonesty therefore can be a legitimate means to an honorable end, and that honorable end is to eradicate the ignorance of Christianity. The spin-off is guilt-free pornography, fornication, and every other sinful pleasure craved by the sin-loving human heart.

Hitchens was wrong. Adolf Hitler *was* a believer in Darwinian evolution. He put survival of the fittest into practice. Hitchens was also either ignorant or he was lying about Darwin and Einstein.[2] Neither of the two were atheists. He did get one out of three correct. Sigmund Freud was an atheist:

> Though Freud hoped that mankind would pass beyond religion, he surely took inspiration from the story of Moses, a figure with whom he had been fascinated for many years. (He published his first essay on the prophet in 1914.) Freud wanted to lead people, and he wanted to make conceptual innovations that had staying power and strength: for this there could be no higher exemplar than the prophet. "Moses and Monotheism" indicates that Freud, irreligious as he was, could still find inspiration in a religious figure. Something similar was true about Freud's predecessor, Nietzsche. Nietzsche is famous for detesting Christianity, and by and large he did. But he did not detest Jesus Christ — whose spontaneity, toughness and freedom of spirit he aspired to emulate. "There has

---

1. http://www.youtube.com/watch?v=bNmSHbMxwL4.
2. See Ray Comfort, *Einstein, God, and the Bible* (Washington, DC: WND Publishing, 2014).

been only one Christian," he once said, one person who truly lived up to the standards of the Gospel, "and he died on the cross."[3]

## The Problem for Atheism

In the BBC documentary "What Happened Before the Big Bang,"[4] a professor asked a group of scientists if they believed that there was something before the Big bang. Most raised their hands. Then the commentator said,

> Ten years ago, this would never have happened. Then, there was no doubt that "before the big bang" made no sense. But today, the certainty has gone. There is no escaping the inconvenient truth that Hubble's graph, work of genius though it is, contains a huge problem. It tells us that everything we see in the universe today — us, trees, galaxies, zebras, emerged in an instant from nothing. And that's a problem. It's all effect, and no cause. The idea of "everything from nothing" is something that has occupied physicist Michio Kaku for much of his professional life.

The physicist then says,

> You know, the idea sounds impossible. Preposterous. I mean, think about it — everything from nothing! The galaxy, the stars in the heavens coming from a pinpoint. I mean how can it be? How can it be that everything comes from nothing? But you know, if you think about it a while, it all depends on how you define "nothing." In Sandusky, Ohio, is Plum Brook Station. It is here that NASA recreates the conditions of space on Earth, and part of that means generating nothing . . . in vast quantities. This is the biggest vacuum chamber in the world. Its eight-feet-thick walls are

---

3. http://www.nytimes.com/2007/09/09/magazine/09wwln-lede-t.html?page-wanted=all.

4. http://www.atheism.kr/bbs/board.php?bo_table=files&wr_id=956&s-fl=&stx=-&sst=wr_ datetime&sod=desc&sop=and&page=3; http://www.bbc.co.uk/ programmes/b00vdkmj.

made from 2,000 tons of solid aluminum. It takes two days of pumping out the air, and another week of freezing out the remaining molecules to create a near-perfect vacuum. A cathedral-sized volume of nothing. When they switch this place on, this is as close as we can get to a state of nothingness. Everywhere we look we see something. We see atoms, we see trees, we see forests, we see water. But hey, right here, we can pump all the atoms out, and this is probably the arena out of which genesis took place. So if you really understand the state of nothing, you understand everything about the origin of the universe.

The commentator then took over from the learned scientist:

Except, of course, it isn't quite that straightforward. For a start, the "nothing" created by NASA still has dimensions — this is nothing in 3-D. And the tests carried out within the chamber can, of course, be viewed. This is nothing through which light can travel. NASA's "nothing" has properties. This "nothing" is, in fact, something.

Many believe such absurdities — that nothing that is something . . . a new and special scientific version of "nothing." In their mind, they think that it gets rid of the unscientific craziness of the "nothing created everything" scenario. An atheist website says,

When physicists say there was "nothing" before the Big Bang of our universe they do not mean literally "nothing." What they mean is that there was no matter, just energy.[5]

It is an intellectual embarrassment to have to point this out to a supposed rational human being, but if "energy" is present, there's not *nothing* at all. There is "energy." Sadly, there are those who believe what atheists say. We received the following email:

A dear friend of mine called me last night absolutely heartbroken, sounding like he had just finished intensely

---

5. "Something from Nothing," http://truth-saves.com/god-doesnt-exist/.

sobbing. His wife, who was once a zealous lover of Jesus, and also a big fan of your ministry, had been slowly slipping from God for about a year. She has spent much of her time feeding her doubts with atheist blogs and has now become a complete skeptic herself. She has cried saying she wants to believe as she used to, but can't anymore. My friend, her husband, is very intelligent and well versed in apologetics and has given her apologetic books, but it seems like nothing he says gets through. My friend is one of the godliest people I know, so was his wife. They have a few children as well. He was calling me for support and advice. Do you have any suggestions on what he should do?

The one thing worse than finding out that a spouse is a false convert, would be *not* finding it out. These atheist bloggers may have done him (and her) a big favor, because Judgment Day will expose every human heart, and then it will be too late.

According to the Bible (and to common sense), atheists are fools who profess to be wise, and their agenda is to reproduce after their own kind. That is where they find a sense of security. They think that stupid is no longer stupid, if enough people believe the stupidity. They point to great intellects such as Carl Sagan (who wasn't an atheist), Albert Einstein (who wasn't an atheist) and Mark Twain (who wasn't an atheist), and with no qualms of conscience say that these men didn't believe in the existence of God.

They will also stand in moral judgment over God by saying that He told Joshua to kill every man, woman, and child, and when you ask them if He *really* did do that, they realize that they have painted themselves into a corner. This is because if God told Joshua to kill the Canaanites, then they are saying that God exists (remember, these are supposed to be atheists), and the issue is really that they are offended by His harsh judgments. If they say that God *doesn't* exist, then God never told Joshua to do anything, because God doesn't exist. And so they are complaining about something that never happened. That's like spending your time complaining that it wasn't fair that Cinderella's slipper didn't fit her ugly sisters.

So anyone who spends their time reading lies written by fools will in time become like them. People who regularly frequent porn sites become porn freaks. Those who bury their heads in violence become violent. Those who spend time in God's Word grow to love and trust God. This issue goes back to Satan's first words to a woman: "Has God said . . . ?" Those who doubt God and instead believe the devil are left with an open invitation to enjoy the pleasures of sin for a season. But they are also left with no purpose in life, no origin *for* life, and no salvation from death and a very real hell.

Early in August 2012, in Huntsville, Alabama, a young man sent a text message to a friend: "I need to quit texting, because I could die in a car accident." While he was finishing the sentence the truck he was driving flew off a cliff, leaving him with a broken neck, a crushed face, a fractured skull, and traumatic brain injuries. His injuries were so serious that doctors had to bring him back to life three times. In an effort to discourage drivers from texting while at the wheel, the state of Alabama decided to fine drivers $25 if they were caught texting.

Actually, I don't believe that the threat of a fine of $25,000,000 would deter teenagers from texting. This is because at that age most of us think we are immortal. It's human nature to think that it's always the other person who gets killed. Such a life philosophy is rooted in arrogance and ignorance, and sadly, that is the spirit behind many in the modern atheist movement.

# CHAPTER FOURTEEN

# WHAT FAITH AIN'T

A professing atheist called recently and asked if we could have lunch together. During the meal he made a strange statement. He said that he didn't have "faith." To him, faith was a belief in something for which there was no solid evidence. He said that he instead had "trust" and "confidence." He was *above* faith.

This common misconception in many modern atheists is often sparked by Mark Twain's thoughtless "Faith is believing what you know ain't so."

So I asked him, "Do you have faith in your wife?" He looked stunned as he began to think of the implications of saying that he didn't. He loved her, so of course he had faith in her. Like a horse and carriage, faith and love go together. If he didn't have faith in his wife, something was seriously wrong with her or their marriage.

As we have already seen, faith for the Christian isn't a shutting of the eyes and, despite all the evidence to the contrary, saying that we have "faith" that some invisible God exists somewhere.

Rather, we *know* that God exists because of the order in nature — from the atom to the amazing order of the universe. We know the Creator exists because all human beings are born with a God-given conscience that is then shaped by the society in which we live. We know He exists because our conscience agrees with His moral Law —the Ten Commandments. We intuitively know that it's wrong to steal, to lie, to murder, and to commit adultery. We know that God exists because we have obeyed His command to repent and trust alone in Jesus for our salvation. In doing so, we have come to know God Himself, and like in any good marriage, we have faith in Him and what He says in His Word. Biblical faith is believing what you know is so.

## Twain's Bitterness

A commentator of Clemens noted:

> As the years went by and he became successful, he became relatively conciliatory toward religion, but as his fortunes reversed late in life, he became bitterly sarcastic and hostile.[1]

This is certainly evident in the following two quotes, written four years before Twain's death:

> Our Bible reveals to us the character of our god with minute and remorseless exactness. . . . It is perhaps the most damnatory biography that exists in print anywhere. It makes Nero an angel of light and leading by contrast.[2]

> There is one notable thing about our Christianity: bad, bloody, merciless, money-grabbing and predatory as it is — in our country particularly, and in all other Christian

---

1. "Mark Twain's Private War with the Almighty," http://www.celebatheists.com/wiki/Mark_Twain.
2. Mark Twain, *Reflections on Religion*, 1906.

countries in a somewhat modified degree — it is still a hundred times better than the Christianity of the Bible, with its prodigious crime — the invention of Hell. Measured by our Christianity of today, bad as it is, hypocritical as it is, empty and hollow as it is, neither the Deity nor His Son is a Christian, nor qualified for that moderately high place. Ours is a terrible religion. The fleets of the world could swim in spacious comfort in the innocent blood it has spilt.[3]

Once again, there are inconsistencies in Twain's condemnation of God. What did God do that was wrong? If evolution is right and we are merely animals, then God's killing of human beings through the Noahic Flood is just an example of Darwinian evolution. The fit survived. Noah and his family made it through the Flood. If God killed the Canaanites through Joshua, the Hebrews were the fit ones who survived and they passed their good genes down to their children. Morals don't come into the equation. That's just the way it is.

If on the other hand it's not an example of evolution, but these are rather examples of murder, who says that it's wrong? Who says that it's morally wrong to take the life of another human being? Is it written in stone somewhere? Who wrote it?

The answer is that the God of the Bible wrote it in stone and passed that Law down to Moses. So Clemens has a problem. His basis for right and wrong comes from the God he accuses of sinning. That's a problem for him because if God is immoral, how can His moral Law be trusted? If God is a murderer, a thief, and a liar, then we can't put any trust is His Ten Commandments. Neither can we have the conviction that it's wrong to steal, lie, or to commit adultery. The Commandments are only as solid as the One who gave them because they are a reflection of His moral character. Mr. Twain then says:

> The Bible is full of interest. It has noble poetry in it; and some clever fables; and some blood-drenched history; and

---

3. Ibid.

some good morals; and a wealth of obscenity; and upwards of a thousand lies. . . . Our Bible reveals to us the character of our god with minute and remorseless exactness. . . . It is perhaps the most damnatory biography that exists in print anywhere. It makes Nero an angel of light and leading by contrast. . . .

Faith is believing something you know ain't true. . . . A man is accepted into a church for what he believes and he is turned out for what he knows. . . . I cannot see how a man of any large degree of humorous perception can ever be religious — unless he purposely shut the eyes of his mind and keep them shut by force. . . . If Christ were here now there is one thing he would not be — a Christian. . . . If there is a God, he is a malign thug.[4]

The Bible certainly is full of interest. It is full or murder, rape, incest, the cutting open of pregnant women, dogs eating people, decapitation, adultery, hatred, lust, fornication, cannibalism, greed, envy, and much more. It is perhaps the most violent history book ever written. The Scriptures don't hide the sins of the sons and daughters of Adam, they expose them and warn that the day will come when God judges every human being for their sinful thoughts and deeds, and that includes the hypocrite.

Look at Twain's cynical tongue: "If Christ were here now there is one thing he would not be — a Christian." What did he mean? Was he saying that he was surrounded by people who didn't live up to the ideal of which Jesus spoke? Did he know some people who professed faith in Jesus and yet played the hypocrite? Then what was stopping him from being a genuine Christian himself? Didn't he read the words of Jesus about taking the log out of our own eye so that we could see clearly? Yet it is clear that he didn't see things clearly because he not only insisted on judging his fellow man, but he insisted on judging Almighty God as falling short of Twain's ideals.

---

4. Mark Twain, *Following the Equator*, chapter 12, http://www.gutenberg.org/files/2895/2895-h/2895-h.htm.

I was once helping Sue with the dishes when I saw a plastic bag hanging on a door handle. I said, "That's quite a good idea actually." When she turned and asked what I was referring to, I said, "The trash bag." It was a good idea because it meant that any smells would be held inside it if the top was tied and it was dropped into the bin. While her back was to me as she washed the dishes I had just dropped some trash into the bag, but I hadn't yet tied the top. She looked at it and said, "That's not a trash bag. It's my lunch!"

God doesn't use the word "trash" to describe false converts that sit within the true Church, but Scripture is close to it. He describes hypocrites as worthless "weeds" and useless "husks," dogs that return to their vomit, and pigs that wallow in filth. He also describes them as "goats." Goats are a type of those who belong to the devil. They will eat anything. So will a false convert. He secretly feeds on the filth of sin, and the day will come when his hypocrisy with be exposed and he will be separated from those whom God has made clean.

It's no wonder Jeremiah was called the "weeping" prophet. I would have wept too if I had to preach his message. He was commissioned by God to tell Israel that He was going to use their enemies to "utterly destroy" them. They had so given themselves to sin that they were without any hope of redemption (see Jeremiah 25:10). God would remove "the voice of the bridegroom, and the voice of the bride." He would eradicate the wondrous joy of marriage and all that comes with it. He would destroy "the sound of the millstone, and the light of the lamp." There would be no food and they would be left in gross darkness (verses 11 and 12).

Poor Jeremiah had to preach a message of wrath, with no good news for his hearers. That should lighten what seems to be a heavy task before us. We are to warn sinners that they have angered God, and that His wrath abides on them (see John 3:36), but we do so for a good reason. We want to diagnose the disease of sin and the consequent judgment, *so that we can joyfully present the cure of the gospel.*

So as Christians we should never be discouraged in our efforts to reach the lost. We speak of the light at the end of the tunnel, and it's not a train heading for us. We have the greatest news that this dark and dying world could ever hope to hear — that Jesus Christ has abolished death and brought life and immortality to light through the gospel (see 2 Timothy 1:10).

**Fearing Heaven**

Again, most atheists pride themselves that they don't have "faith." But look at how two other founding fathers of modern atheism based their whole life's philosophy on a blind faith. Bertrand Russell "believed" that when he died, his body would corrupt and that nothing else would live on. That was his belief. That's where he placed his faith . . . having nothing to base it on, unless he had some sort of unique insight into the afterlife (notice the word "believe" in his quote):

> I believe that when I die I shall rot, and nothing of my ego will survive. I am not young and I love life. But I should scorn to shiver with terror at the thought of annihilation. Happiness is nonetheless true happiness because it must come to an end, nor do thought and love lose their value because they are not everlasting. Many a man has borne himself proudly on the scaffold; surely the same pride should teach us to think truly about man's place in the world. Even if the open windows of science at first make us shiver after the cozy indoor warmth of traditional humanizing myths, in the end the fresh air brings vigor, and the great spaces have a splendor of their own.[5]

Professing atheist Isaac Asimov, also had a blind faith (again, notice the word "believe"):

> I don't believe in an afterlife, so I don't have to spend my whole life fearing hell, or fearing heaven even more. For whatever the tortures of hell, I think the boredom of heaven would be even worse.[6]

---

5. https://www.goodreads.com/quotes/28449-i-believe-that-when-i-die-i-shall-rot-and.

6. http://www.brainyquote.com/quotes/quotes/i/isaacasimo122403.html.

With no evidence upon which to base his faith, he said that he didn't believe in the afterlife. That was his belief. He was so full of faith that it got rid of his fear of heaven. His fear needn't have been of boredom. If heaven exists, then God exists, and if God exists, Mr. Asimov, like the rest of us who die without a Savior, is in big trouble.

Physicist Michio Kaku said,

> Speaking as a scientist I think that there is a problem with regards to the afterlife and religious immortality, and that is there is no proof that it exists. Remarkable claims require remarkable proof. But maybe you don't need proof. Well I do.[7]

Mr. Kaku should change his wording a little so that he wouldn't be construed as a dogmatist. His presupposition is that there is no proof for everlasting life, so as far as he is concerned, there is no need for a moment of investigation. But more than that, Mr. Kaku reveals ignorance as to the fantastic nature of his claim. In saying "There is no proof," he claims an attribute of God. He is omniscient. He knows everything in the universe. All knowledge is his. He knows that there is no proof anywhere of an afterlife. Rather, to speak as a true scientist, he should say that he hasn't found any proof of the afterlife. Of course, the normal atheist comeback is that we can't say that Santa doesn't exist. Somewhere in the universe he and his staff may be making toys and eyeing chimneys. However, believing whether Santa does or does not exist has no relevance to your eternal destiny. If you close your mind to eternity and the salvation of God, your decision to do so will produce eternal remorse.

I saw an advertisement recently where cameras were set up to watch a supermarket shopper's reaction to a scenario. Just as he was about to go through the checkout, a man who had a single item asked if he could step in front of him. Of course, the shopper kindly let him go first. Suddenly balloons dropped from the roof and music began to play — because the man he let through won $50,000 for

---

7. "Michio Kaku on Life After Death, Creationism and Scientific Evidence of Geological Time," www.youtube.com/watch?v=z-sBp4D9dMU.

being the one-millionth shopper. The camera then zoomed in on the shopper's look of unbelief.

Of course this was just a setup and it was fascinating to watch his response. The intrigue probably comes because of our ability to identify with someone being that close to winning big and missing out.

Pete Best was the member of the Beatles who was dropped just before the music group exploded across the world, making the other members millionaires overnight. They were stacking platinum albums as he stacked loaves of bread in a delivery van in a factory. He was close, but he missed out.

Many are like that when it comes to getting to heaven. They believe in God, perhaps go to church, own a Bible or two, but they've never been born again. They are close, but they are in danger of missing out — not on mere money, but on eternal life. Horrible as that may be, it's not the real tragedy. If they die in their sins, they will not only miss the eternal pleasures of heaven, they will find themselves damned in a terrible place called "hell."

# CHAPTER FIFTEEN

# FATHER OF MERCIES

"If Christ were here now there is one thing he would not be — a Christian." Mark Twain[1]

I am forever amazed at how the Scriptures pinpoint our motives. If you want proof that the Bible is inspired, study it. Don't go to skeptics' websites and believe what they say, or read verses about the atrocities of men in Scripture, or the frightening harsh judgments of God. Study Scripture for yourself. Do a "subject" study. Follow what the Bible says about one particular subject — for example, the sinful nature of man, the place of blood in redemption, the issue of faith, and 101 other subjects. Keep in mind that the Bible was written over a 1,500-year period, and that it was penned by 40 or so different authors from all walks of life, and you will be forced

---

1. *Mark Twain's Notebook*, http://www.twainquotes.com/Christianity.html.

into the conclusion that each of them were inspired by God, as the Scriptures maintain they were.[2]

Here is Mark Twain's heart-motive for hating the God of the Bible: "He who walks in his uprightness fears the LORD, but he who is perverse in his ways despises Him" (Proverbs 14:2).

I recently met a man named "Ever." He was in his early twenties and was at our ministry fixing our Internet server. I gave him a copy of our "180" pro-life video and asked him if he thought that there was an afterlife. When he enthusiastically said that he did, I asked him if he was a Christian. He again responded with a wholehearted "Yes!" But when I asked further I found that he hadn't been born again. I explained the new birth, saying that the difference between someone who was born again and someone who wasn't, was like the difference between a man who is wearing a parachute and one who isn't. They both seem to be in the same state, until they jump 10,000 feet out of the plane. I then took him through the Ten Commandments and explained the Cross. He was very grateful, so I gave him my book *Out of the Comfort Zone* and took delight in signing it, "For Ever. . . ."

A short time later he approached me and asked where he could find a certain place in our building. As I began to explain which doors he should go through, I stood up from my chair and said, "Why don't I just take you there, so that you won't get lost!"

The desire of every Christian should be to stop whatever we are doing to take sinners to the foot of the Cross. That's what I did for Ever, and those of us who have already been saved will be forever grateful that someone took us by the hand to explain the wonderful truths of the gospel. That's what I would like to do for you later on in this chapter, if you have never been born again.

**More Criticizing of God**

After railing on God for not coming up to his standards of moral conduct, Mark Twain says,

> And now you know, by these sure indications, what happened under the personal direction of the Father of

2. 2 Timothy 3:16.

Mercies in his Midianite campaign. The Minnesota campaign was merely a duplicate of the Midianite raid. Nothing happened in the one that didn't happen in the other.

No, that is not strictly true. The Indian was more merciful than was the Father of Mercies. He sold no virgins into slavery to minister to the lusts of the murderers of their kindred while their sad lives might last; he raped them, then charitably made their subsequent sufferings brief, ending them with the precious gift of death. He burned some of the houses, but not all of them. He carried out innocent dumb brutes, but he took the lives of none.[3]

Twain sarcastically calls God "the Father of Mercies," not understanding the nature of mercy. Mercy is extended when God doesn't treat us with justice. Mercy is when we get what we don't deserve. This is perhaps the greatest error of the ungodly. They have no understanding of the righteousness, holiness, or the justice of God. If He treated us according to our sins, we would be in big trouble, and such a thought leads us to our salvation.

Perhaps you consider yourself to be a spiritual person, and you have been living your life doing the best you can. Like Mark Twain, you believe in God. You do kind things for others when you can. You confess your sins, but you have never been "born again." Again, this is an extremely important matter because (as we have seen) Jesus warned that those who are not born again can't enter the kingdom of heaven.

So let's make sure that you make it to heaven, because in the light of eternity, nothing else really matters. We will look to the Law of God and let it examine you by putting you on the stand and letting its light expose what you are before the Day of Judgment. This may not be a pleasant experience, but it is a most necessary one. So here goes. . . .

Have you ever lied? Do yourself a big favor — don't try and soften the question by talking about "white" lies or "fibs" or telling

3. *Letters from the Earth*, "Letter XI," by Mark Twain, http://www.classicreader.com/book/1930/12/

Aunt Martha that you liked her hat when it was horrible. Simply answer the question. Have you ever told an untruth, "Yes or no?" Have you stolen anything in your life? Again, don't talk about candy as a kid. Have you ever taken something that belonged to another person, irrespective of its size or value? Yes or no? Have you ever used God's name in vain (failed to give it honor, used it lightly or in place of a cuss word), even once? Have you ever looked with lust (sexual desire) or hated anyone? If you have done any of these things, then you are a self-admitted lying thief, a blasphemer, a murderer, or an adulterer at heart.

So what do you have to say for yourself? How can you justify murder, adultery, lying, stealing, and using God's name as a cuss word? Confessing your sins can't help you. That is like standing before a judge and *confessing* that you are guilty as charged. How can that help? Saying you are sorry and that you won't do it again won't help either. Of course, a criminal should be sorry, and of course he shouldn't commit the crimes again. So what are you going to say to make things right? How can you avoid being guilty on Judgment Day and not be justly damned in a terrible place called "hell"?

Every one of us has more than a skeleton in the closet. It's more like a city graveyard. Jeremiah 17:1 says, "The sin of Judah is written with a pen of iron; with the point of a diamond it is engraved on the tablet of their heart. . . ." We need only to check the table of our own heart to know the truth of this. A certain food smell or a few bars of a tune can bring instant recall of an event that took place in our life many years ago. The conscious mind may have pushed the sinful things we have done aside temporarily, but every sin we have ever committed is locked up in a vault of the memory banks. It will be unlocked on the Day of Judgment and be evidence that will damn those who are found in their sins. I am terrified beyond words for you. A reviewer of the *Autobiography of Mark Twain* said,

> But while the autobiography contains many such bare-knuckle outbursts, you won't find many revelations about Twain's inner moral struggles. Three months into the dictations, he says, "I have thought of 1,500 or 2,000

incidents in my life which I am ashamed of, but I have not gotten one of them to consent to go on paper yet."[4]

I have to admit that I have a sense of admiration for Twain — that he would even admit to having that many incidents in his life of which he is ashamed. That shows that he still had a semblance of conscience. But honesty won't save us. It just means that the criminal admits his guilt. So don't take consolation in admitting your sins or even having a sense of regret about them. Everything of which we should be ashamed — every immoral deed, every unclean thought, every lie, blasphemy, idle talk, theft, fornication — every transgression against that perfect Law is written on the tablet of the heart, and is waiting, "kept in store" for that Day. Don't die in your sins. Let the voice of your conscience expose it. But don't be like Mr. Twain and stay in the darkness. Bring it to the light. Confess and forsake it, because, as the old hymn says, "There's room at the cross."

We tend to look at sin using the world's moral standards. We think that lying is wrong because it betrays trust. Stealing is wrong because it destroys society. Homosexual adoption is said to be wrong by many people because children need a mother and a father. If the "morality" of something is based on what works and what doesn't, then we just need to find a way to have a relationship that works if lies are told. Or stealing becomes morally okay if no one notices that they have been ripped off. Or if children raised by homosexuals are proven to be stable and happy, then the lifestyle becomes acceptable. Rather, sin is wrong because God says it's wrong.

All of us have seriously sinned against our Creator; we are under His wrath and we *can't* help ourselves. All we can do is raise our hands in surrender. This is where the new birth comes in.

A Protestant or Roman Catholic, or any religious person who is not born again, is almost certainly trusting in their own goodness or their own religious "works" to save them on Judgment Day. They are hoping that their praying, fasting, repentance, "good"

---

4. http://www.independent.co.uk/arts-entertainment/books/news/after-keeping-us-waiting-for-a-century-mark-twain-will-finally-reveal-all-1980695.html    Harriet E. Smith, editor, *Autobiography of Mark Twain*, Vol. 1 (Berkeley, CA: University of California Press).

works, etc., will give them a pass into heaven. However, Christians are sinful people who trust alone in the person of Jesus Christ for their eternal salvation. This is because the Law has shown them that their good works aren't "good." They suddenly understand that in God's eyes they are criminals and that He is a perfect judge. Therefore, anything they offer Him isn't good at all. It's an attempt to bribe Him to dismiss their case. It would be infinitely easier to floss the back teeth of the lions at your local zoo (at feeding time) than to bribe God by your religious works. Or let me put it another way to get the point across. It would be far easier for a blindfolded double amputee to leap across the widest part of the Grand Canyon than to cause God to look the other way because of your religious works.

If you are unsaved, you are hopelessly joined to sin and death. No amount of religious wrestling will get you away from it. If you want to live, you have no other choice than to rip yourself away from sin, through the act of God-given repentance and trust in Jesus. You and I can't even come to Christ without the hand of God guiding us and His Holy Spirit drawing us to Him. Jesus said that no one can come to the Son unless the Father draws him (see John 6:44).

In the epic movie *Ben Hur*, Judah was a galley slave. He had been unjustly doomed and sent to die as a slave of Rome. However, because he reminded the new commander of his son who had been killed in battle, the commander took pity on him.

As they headed into a battle, the commander gave instructions that a chain was not to be threaded through Ben Hur's ankle ring. The practice of securing the slaves to the ship ensured there would be a commitment to rowing during the battle, because if the ship went down, so did they.

During the ferocious encounter, the ship was rammed and began to sink. The slaves cried out in panic and tried to rip the chain from their ankle rings, cutting into their bloodied flesh.

The unchained Ben Hur was the only slave who could leave the ship. However, instead of saving himself, he overpowered the guard who held the keys, and released the condemned and helpless prisoners.

There was only One who was free from the chains of sin and death — Jesus of Nazareth. But instead of saving Himself, He went for the one with the keys, and said, "I am he who lives, and was dead, and, behold, I am alive forevermore. Amen. And I have the keys of Hades and of Death" (Revelation 1:18).

Through His death and Resurrection, He removed the chains of sin and death from the human race. Now all we need to do is tell the lost to get up and save themselves (by the grace of God) from the sinking ship:

> And with many other words he testified and exhorted them, saying, "Be saved from this perverse generation" (Acts 2:40).

So, do you believe me? Or do you think that I am melodramatic when I'm raving about you being in danger? Then listen to this:

> A woman's car broke down late one moonless night in an unfamiliar area. She was afraid, so she wound the vehicle's windows up tight, locked the doors, and turned on the car radio to keep her company. She decided that it would be wise to wait until the morning light before going for help.
>
> A short time later a frantic man appeared at her window and began to yell at her. Frightened, she gestured for him to go away. He left and then returned seconds later with a rock in his hand, smashed the window of her car, and pulled her out, much to the woman's horrified protests.
>
> As they fell to the ground a massive train slammed into her car, causing it to burst into flames.

You may consider Christians to be raving lunatics, but all we are frantically trying to do is warn you that you are in terrible danger. The train of God's moral Law is merciless. Your ignorance of the imminent peril doesn't make it disappear. Please, soften your heart and listen before it is too late.

Fortunately, the Bible tells us that God is "rich in mercy."[5] Jesus portrayed Him as a loving Father who is looking out for the return of his prodigal son. Here's the story from Luke 15:

> And not many days after, the younger son gathered all together, journeyed to a far country, and there wasted his possessions with prodigal living. But when he had spent all, there arose a severe famine in that land, and he began to be in want. Then he went and joined himself to a citizen of that country, and he sent him into his fields to feed swine. And he would gladly have filled his stomach with the pods that the swine ate, and no one gave him anything. But when he came to himself, he said, "How many of my father's hired servants have bread enough and to spare, and I perish with hunger! I will arise and go to my father, and will say to him, 'Father, I have sinned against heaven and before you, and I am no longer worthy to be called your son. Make me like one of your hired servants.' "

And that's what he did. He went back to his father who was waiting for his return. His father saw him coming, "had compassion, and ran and fell on his neck and kissed him." That's a "type" of the sinner coming to God. So here's an important question. Do you know why he went to a far country? He went there to spend his money on "prodigal living." That's the biblical equivalent of "wild parties." But parties don't cost that much. Prostitutes do. He wanted to have sex. I know this because the Bible tells me so (verse 30): "But as soon as this son of yours came, who has devoured your livelihood with harlots. . . ."

That's why he went as far away from his father as he could. And that's what happens to us when we engage in illicit sex. Just like Mark Twain, we want to get as far away from the God of the Bible as we can . . . and in our minds the furthest we can get is atheism. If God doesn't exist, then anything goes — there's no right or wrong. The other popular way to get away from God is to be an idolater. That was Twain's sin, and more than likely yours and mine.

---

5. Ephesians 2:4.

When the father saw his beloved son at a distance, he ran to him, fell upon him, and kissed him. Think of it. Jesus is saying that you are the prodigal, and God is that father. Add to that what He did to save guilty sinners from damnation in hell — He became a human being, so that He could pay our fine, so that we could leave the courtroom. That's what took place on that terrible Cross 2,000 years ago. The sin of the world fell upon the innocent Lamb of God — He was bruised for *our* iniquities. The sweetest words that any human being will ever hear will be the words "Not guilty." Those who are free from guilt on that terrible day will live.

Look at the following portion of Scripture and notice the repetition of the words "only begotten":

> And the Word was made flesh, and dwelt among us, (and we beheld his glory, the glory as of the only begotten of the Father,) full of grace and truth. . . . No man hath seen God at any time, the only begotten Son, which is in the bosom of the Father, he hath declared him. . . . For God so loved the world, that he gave his only begotten Son, that whosoever believeth in him should not perish, but have everlasting life. . . . He that believeth on him is not condemned: but he that believeth not is condemned already, because he hath not believed in the name of the only begotten Son of God (John 1:14–3:18; KJV).

The words "only begotten" mean that Jesus was absolutely unique. He was the only One who could pay for the sin of the world because He was morally perfect, and He was morally perfect because He was God in human form. And He proved this by not only suffering for our sins, but by resurrecting Himself from the dead:

> "Therefore My Father loves Me, because I lay down My life that I may take it again. No one takes it from Me, but I lay it down of Myself. I have power to lay it down, and I have power to take it again. This command I have received from My Father" (John 10:17–18).

So what are you going to do? Are you going to stay religious, trusting in yourself, or are you going to obey God's command for you to repent, surrender to the Savior, and trust in Him alone so that God can clothe you in the righteousness of Jesus Christ? *Please* surrender. Give up the battle. Do it now because you may not have tomorrow. Confess your sins to God and then turn from them. He will help you. And then make sure that your trust is in Jesus Christ alone. Transfer your trust from yourself to the Savior. If you are not sure what to say, pray a prayer similar to the one King David prayed after his sin was exposed. He committed adultery and murder, and after his sin was exposed, he cried:

> Have mercy upon me, O God, according to Your lovingkindness; according to the multitude of Your tender mercies, blot out my transgressions. Wash me thoroughly from my iniquity, and cleanse me from my sin. For I acknowledge my transgressions, and my sin is always before me. Against You, You only, have I sinned, and done this evil in Your sight — That You may be found just when You speak, and blameless when You judge. Behold, I was brought forth in iniquity, and in sin my mother conceived me. Behold, You desire truth in the inward parts, and in the hidden part You will make me to know wisdom. Purge me with hyssop, and I shall be clean; wash me, and I shall be whiter than snow. Make me hear joy and gladness, that the bones You have broken may rejoice. Hide Your face from my sins, and blot out all my iniquities. Create in me a clean heart, O God, and renew a steadfast spirit within me (Psalm 51:1–10).

If Mark Twain had looked at his own morality with the critical eye he used to look at God's morality, he would have fallen at the feet of His mercy, found forgiveness of sins, and everlasting life. If he had studied Scripture with a humble heart instead of trying to justify his own sins by looking for sin in God, he would have seen Scripture addresses the subject:

Therefore listen to me, you men of understanding: Far be it from God to do wickedness, and from the Almighty to commit iniquity. For He repays man according to his work, and makes man to find a reward according to his way. Surely God will never do wickedly, nor will the Almighty pervert justice. Who gave Him charge over the earth? Or who appointed Him over the whole world? If He should set His heart on it, if He should gather to Himself His Spirit and His breath, all flesh would perish together, and man would return to dust (Job 34:10–15).

But instead of humbly seeking God, Twain turns his poisonous pen on Jesus:

Would you expect this same conscienceless God, this moral bankrupt, to become a teacher of morals; of gentleness; of meekness; of righteousness; of purity? It looks impossible, extravagant; but listen to him. These are his own words:

"Blessed are the poor in spirit, for theirs is the kingdom of heaven.

Blessed are they that mourn, for they shall be comforted.

Blessed are the meek, for they shall inherit the earth.

Blessed are they which do hunger and thirst after righteousness, for they shall be filled.

*Blessed are the merciful*, for they shall obtain mercy.

Blessed are the pure in heart, for they shall see God.

*Blessed are the peacemakers*, for they shall be called the children of God.

Blessed arc they which are persecuted for righteousness' sake, for theirs is the kingdom of heaven. Blessed are ye, when men shall revile you, and persecute you, and say all manner of evil against you falsely, for my sake."

The mouth that uttered these immense sarcasms, these giant hypocrisies, is the very same that ordered the wholesale massacre of the Midianitish men and babies and cattle; the wholesale destruction of house and city; the wholesale banishment of the virgins into a filthy and unspeakable slavery. This is the same person who brought upon the Midianites the fiendish cruelties which were repeated by the red Indians, detail by detail, in Minnesota eighteen centuries later. The Midianite episode filled him with joy. So did the Minnesota one, or he would have prevented it.

The Beatitudes and the quoted chapters from Numbers and Deuteronomy ought always to be read from the pulpit together; then the congregation would get an all-round view of Our Father in Heaven. Yet not in a single instance have I ever known a clergyman to do this.[6]

In 1878, Twain wrote, "I don't believe one word of your Bible was inspired by God any more than I believe any other book. I believe it is the work of man from beginning to end — atonement and all."[7] If that's true, there seems to be a huge disconnect here. He said of Jesus:

This is the same person who brought upon the Midianites the fiendish cruelties which were repeated by the red Indians, detail by detail, in Minnesota eighteen centuries later.[8]

Yet, I repeat, he doesn't believe a word of the Bible. Why then does he accuse God of immoral acts when he doesn't believe that the immoral acts took place? If the Old Testament was a fable, a mere history book, embellishing stories that never took place, then he has no case against God.

Why does he say that Jesus was the God of Moses in human form? Does he believe all the Old Testament prophecies about Jesus

---

6. *Letters from the Earth*, "Letter XI," by Mark Twain, http://www.classicreader.com/book/1930/12/.

7. Edgar Lee Masters, *Mark Twain: A Portrait* (New York: Biblo and Tannen, 1966 [c1938]), p. 143.

8. Ibid.

of Nazareth being God in the flesh? If he doesn't, why did he say that Jesus is the God that was so cruel to the Midianites, because Twain believes He wasn't. In his desperate effort to impugn God, Mark Twain revealed his personal animosity toward the God who gave him life.

> If I could, I would make such havoc among the shams of Palestine that I would leave little there for men to feast their eyes and feed their fancies upon save the Hill of Calvary, and the lesson it carries to the most careless heart that pulses in its presence. I would leave it to tell of Him who suffered there, and to suggest the picture of the Crucifixion more vividly than the multitude of its surroundings, which are at best of questionable holiness, can ever do. All things must pass away but that one Figure, and when they do, the world will be none the loser for it. . . . the Teacher of Nazareth, standing upon the height of Calvary — sacred because the theatre of the noblest self-sacrifice man has yet conceived — shall say to them that mourn this desolation, "Peace! I am the Resurrection and the Life!"[9]

> Jesus died to save men — a small thing for an immortal to do, and didn't save many, anyway; but if he had been damned for the race that would have been act of a size proper to a god, and would have saved the whole race. However, why should anybody want to save the human race, or damn it either? Does God want its society? Does Satan?[10]

In the Book of Genesis, God said, "Let there be light." Genesis is itself a light. If it is believed, then we are given light on many other subjects, including suffering, pain, and death. If we don't believe it, we are left in the dark as to why these things exist.

It is evident that Mark Twain had left the light off when he spoke of God and suffering. Those who believe the account of the Genesis creation believe that when God made man, everything was

---

9. Mark Twain, *Who Is Mark Twain?* "I Rise to a Question of Privilege."
10. Notebook #42, www.twainquotes.com/Jesus.html.

good. There were no earthquakes, tornados, hurricanes, cancer, disease, and death. There were no disease-ridden mosquitoes, man-eating sharks and tigers, and vicious poisonous snakes that lashed out at man. *Everything* was good.

> There is no other life; life itself is only a vision and a dream for nothing exists but space and you. If there was an all-powerful God, he would have made all good, and no bad.[11]

For some reason, Twain is deaf to Scripture. Didn't he read that God made everything good? He who rejects "In the beginning" leaves himself with no beginning, no end, and no reason to be in-between. Or was it that the Scriptures say that after God made all things sin entered the human race, and He cursed the earth and thus we have all these terrible things. Pain, suffering, and death exist because man is evil, and the best of us, if treated justly, would be in hell in an instant. It seems that there is no argument from Mr. Twain about man being evil:

> Of all the creatures that were made, man is the most detestable. Of the entire brood he is the only one — the solitary one — that possesses malice. That is the basest of all instincts, passions, vices — the most hateful. He is the only creature that has pain for sport, knowing it to be pain. Also — in all the lists he is the only creature that has a nasty mind.[12]

Here is the self-delusion of self-righteousness and the blindness of sin. Twain's eye was quick to see sin in God and man, but not in himself to a point of repentance. Despite this, God has already shown Himself to be rich in mercy, and has treated us kindly by giving us life, color, beauty, love, and laughter. He has lavished His goodness upon us and given us the warmth of the sun, fruit trees, the oceans to fish in, snow to sky on, and mountains to climb. On top of all this, He provided a way for each of us to have everlasting

11. Mark Twain, *Mark Twain in Eruption* (New York: Harper, 1940).
12. Smith, *Autobiography of Mark Twain*.

life, with pleasure forevermore. But Mark Twain ignores all of God's kindness, and in his ignorance reveals even more disdain for his Creator:

> I will tell you a pleasant tale which has in it a touch of pathos. A man got religion, and asked the priest what he must do to be worthy of his new estate. The priest said, "imitate our Father in Heaven, learn to be like Him." The man studied his Bible diligently and thoroughly and understandingly, and then with prayers for heavenly guidance instituted his imitations. He tricked his wife into falling downstairs, and she broke her back and became a paralytic for life; he betrayed his brother into the hands of a sharper, who robbed him of his all and landed him in the almshouse; he inoculated one son with hookworms, another with the sleeping sickness, another with gonorrhea; he furnished one daughter with scarlet fever and ushered her into her teens deaf, dumb, and blind for life; and after helping a rascal seduce the remaining one, he closed his doors against her and she died in a brothel cursing him. Then he reported to the priest, who said that THAT was no way to imitate his Father in Heaven! The convert asked wherein he had failed, but the priest changed the subject and inquired what kind of weather he was having, up his way.[13]

And so those who love their sins love Mark Twain. They feel justified in their wickedness because he gives them ammunition to fire at heaven.

It is very difficult to reason with a man who believes that he's an atheist. His worldview pins a notice on his head saying, "I'm unreasonable." Fortunately, most who believe they are atheists are not. An atheist, by definition, is omniscient. He knows that God doesn't exist. All knowledge is his. To him, nowhere in the universe is evidence that God exists. So when pressed a little, most who think they are atheists adjust a little and admit to being agnostic in

---

13. Mark Twain, *Letters from the Earth* (New York: Harper & Row, 1942), p. 39.

worldview. They don't know if God exists because they don't have access to all knowledge. Mark Twain knew that God existed, and he believed portions of the Bible, evidenced by the scorn he had for the One portrayed in its pages. Insightful though he was into the hypocrisy of those around him, he didn't have insight enough to realize that "our Christianity" was made up of evil men and women who used it for their own ends.

It seems that Mr. Twain eventually became some sort of a believer in Darwinian evolution. He believed that man was a primate rather than that he was made in the image of God, according to the Book of Genesis. This leaves him with a quandary that still mystifies modern evolutionary believers. Why is man interested in God? None of the "other" animals are preoccupied with searching for their Creator. David said of the Scriptures, "Your Word is a lamp to my feet and a light to my path" (Psalm 119:105). Mark Twain had no lamp. His path was one of darkness by his own choosing. He surmises:

> Man is a Religious Animal. Man is the only Religious Animal. He is the only animal that has the True Religion — several of them. He is the only animal that loves his neighbor as himself and cuts his throat if his theology isn't straight. He has made a graveyard of the globe in trying his honest best to smooth his brother's path to happiness and heaven. . . . The higher animals have no religion. And we are told that they are going to be left out in the Hereafter. I wonder why? It seems questionable taste.[14]

Man is not an animal. He is a moral being, made in the image of God. Again, this is the reason why Twain railed on God. It was because God had given him the ability to make moral judgments. His problem was that he judged everyone except himself. He judged Christians, hypocrites, and politicians. Man was "detestable." And as we have seen many times, he even judged Almighty God. It seems he skipped over Romans chapter two:

---

14. Mark Twain, "The Lowest Animal essay, 1897," in *Letters from the Earth*.

Therefore you are inexcusable, O man, whoever you are who judge, for in whatever you judge another you condemn yourself; for you who judge practice the same things. But we know that the judgment of God is according to truth against those who practice such things. And do you think this, O man, you who judge those practicing such things, and doing the same, that you will escape the judgment of God? Or do you despise the riches of His goodness, forbearance, and longsuffering, not knowing that the goodness of God leads you to repentance? But in accordance with your hardness and your impenitent heart you are treasuring up for yourself wrath in the day of wrath and revelation of the righteous judgment of God, who "will render to each one according to his deeds": eternal life to those who by patient continuance in doing good seek for glory, honor, and immortality; but to those who are self-seeking and do not obey the truth, but obey unrighteousness — indignation and wrath, tribulation and anguish, on every soul of man who does evil, of the Jew first and also of the Greek; but glory, honor, and peace to everyone who works what is good, to the Jew first and also to the Greek. For there is no partiality with God (Romans 2:1–11).

Mark Twain went to meet his Maker on April 21, 1910 in Redding, Connecticut, of angina pectoris. Upon hearing of Twain's death of a heart attack, President Taft said,

Mark Twain gave pleasure — real intellectual enjoyment — to millions, and his works will continue to give such pleasure to millions yet to come. . . . His humor was American, but he was nearly as much appreciated by Englishmen and people of other countries as by his own countrymen. He has made an enduring part of American literature.

Many years ago when I was in New Zealand, I was driving up a mountain with my family when we stopped for a break. As I stretched my legs, I noticed a tiny tree growing in the soil by the edge of the road. A seed had obviously dropped from a tree and taken root. I carefully scooped it up in my hands and later that day planted it in our garden. It eventually grew to about 15 feet and stood as a stark reminder that I had stolen it.

"But," you say, "that tree was owned by the people of New Zealand. It wasn't theft." If that is true, can I then go to a public forest and dig up a few trees for my yard, and while I'm there take a truck load of soil? Of course not. If I did that I would be arrested for theft. I'm sure it's the same in any country. No one, not even the president of a country, has the right to take a tree, a load of soil, or even a few rocks from public land. So when it comes down to it, we "the people" don't really own a thing. There's only one rightful owner: "The earth is the LORD's, and the fullness thereof; the world, and they that dwell therein" (Psalm 24:1; KJV).

The other lesson I learned is that (in time) small sins grow into big sins. That's what happened with the brilliant Mark Twain. Not long after he went to meet his Maker, Twain's family held back some of his writings that could have been considered irreverent toward traditional religion. One of these works was *Letters from the Earth*, which was published in 1962 when his daughter Clara changed her mind in response to criticism regarding her withholding it.[15] The very anti-God *The Mysterious Stranger* was released back in 1916. *Little Bessie*, the story that ridiculed Christianity, was first released in the 1972 collection *Mark Twain's Fables of Man*.[16]

Those who were close to him have said that Mark Twain often thought about the subject of life after death. His daughter Clara, said, "Sometimes he believed death ended everything, but most of the time he felt sure of a life beyond."[17]

---

15. Arthur Gelb, "Anti-Religious Work by Twain, Long Withheld, to Be Published," *The New York Times*, August 24, 1962, p. 23, ISSN 0362-4331, retrieved 4/22/2008.

16. John S. Tuckey, Kenneth M. Sanderson, Bernard L. Stein, and Frederick Anderson, editors, *Mark Twain's Fables of Man* (Berkeley, CA: University of California Press, 1972), "Little Bessie."

17. William E. Phipps, *Mark Twain's Religion* (Macon, GA: Mercer University Press, 2003), p. 304.

Mark Twain has left us. He now knows that there is life after death. However, you are still on this earth. You haven't yet passed into eternity. So let me share an experience I had in May 2014. I was honored to speak at a prayer breakfast with 250 dignitaries. I sat next to a very dignified-looking council-man who said that he went to a traditional church. However, I gathered (from a word he let slip) that he was a stranger to the new birth.

Twain's daughter Clara Clemens
(Photo courtesy of Library of Congress)

Just as I was about to get up and speak he gave me his business card, so I gave him mine (it was a humorous card). He looked closely at it for a moment, gave a big smile and said, "I *really* like you." I thought, "You're not going to like me in about 30 minutes."

For the next half hour I preached my heart out, explaining how no one can earn everlasting life, because we are criminals in God's sight, and that the only thing that can save us from a very real hell is God's mercy.

As I sat back down I whispered, "Do you still like me?"

He soberly replied, "God will not be bribed. It took 30 minutes for me to get it, but I get it. God will not be bribed!"

I signed one of my books and slid it across to him. He looked almost stern and for a second I thought I had gone too far, but he then said, "Thank you." Tears welled in his eyes, and he added, "Thank you . . . more than you will ever know." It was a very moving moment and one that I will never forget.

I hope that after reading this book, you are saying, "I get it."

We can believe God and groan as we wait for the new heavens and the new earth, or we can join Mark Twain and just groan in anguish and futility, because we don't have any hope of deliverance. His last written statement — a hopeless statement — was,

> Death, the only immortal who treats us all alike, whose pity and whose peace and whose refuge are for all — the soiled and the pure, the rich and the poor, the loved and the unloved.

According to Scripture, Mr. Clemens was blind. The god of this world had blinded his mind because he refused to come to the only One who could give him sight. His blindness was willful because he loved his sin. He loved darkness more than light. I pray that the same is not true of you.

Editorial drawing from the *Baltimore American*, April 23, 1910, following Mark Twain's death, featuring a grieving Uncle Sam, and quoting the Bible Twain so despised (Ecclesiastes 3:4).

For a complete list of books by Ray Comfort go to www.livingwaters.com.

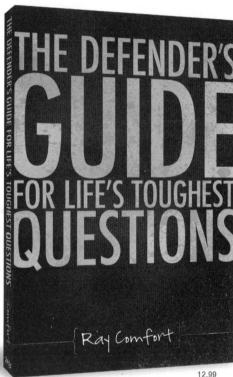